M000105265

SUPERb Woman

From Bad Girl to God's Girl

By

Dr. Patrice J. Carter

SUPERb Woman
From Bad Girl to God's Girl
Copyright © 2011 Dr. Patrice J. Carter

Scripture is taken from *GOD'S WORD®*. Copyright 1995 God's Word to the Nations. Used by permission of Baker Publishing Group. All rights reserved.
Scriptures taken from *The Message*. Copyright © 1993, 1994, 1995, 1996, 2000, 2001, 2002. Used by permission of NavPress Publishing Group.
Scriptures, unless otherwise indicated, are taken from the Holy Bible: New International Version. Copyright © 1973, 1978, 1984 by International Bible Society. Used by permission of Zondervan.
Spirit-Filled Life Bible, Copyright© 1991 by Thomas Nelson, Inc.; The Holy Bible, New King James Version. Copyright © 1982 by Thomas Nelson, Inc.; The New King James Bible, New Testament Copyright © 1979 by Thomas Nelson, Inc.; The New King James Bible, New Testament and Psalms Copyright © 1980 by Thomas Nelson, Inc.
Scripture quotations taken from the Amplified® Bible,
Copyright © 1954, 1958, 1962, 1964, 1965, 1987 by The Lockman Foundation
Used by permission. (www.Lockman.org)
Scripture quotations are taken from the Holy Bible, New Living Translation, Copyright ©1996, 2004, 2007 by Tyndale House Foundation. Used by permission of Tyndale House Publishers, Inc., Carol Stream, Illinois 60188. All rights reserved.
Scripture quotations taken from the New American Standard Bible®, Copyright © 1960, 1962, 1963, 1968, 1971, 1972, 1973, 1975, 1977, 1995 by The Lockman Foundation. Used by permission." (www.Lockman.org).
The Holy Bible: English Standard Version, Scripture quotations marked "ESV" are taken from The Holy Bible: English Standard Version, copyright © 2001, Wheaton: Good News Publishers. Used by permission. All rights reserved.

The World English Bible is a Modern English update of the American Standard Version of 1901. The translation and review is currently in progress, so please check back from time to time for updates. This translation is in the Public Domain, so feel free to copy, publish (for free or for a price), and use it. You don't need to pay any royalties or even to ask for any additional permission. You already have permission to publish, copy, and distribute the World English Bible as much as you want to in any form (spoken, written, paper, electronic, etc.). We do ask that you update your copy that you publish periodically until the World English Bible editing is done, as a courtesy to your readers (and not as a requirement). If you make any changes to the text of the World English Bible, we do ask that you not call it the World English Bible any more, to avoid confusion, unless you get specific permission from us to do so.
31 Epitome: A Poem for Mertyse. By Carrie Elliott. Printed with permission.

ISBN: 978-0-9741406-9-8

Library of Congress Control Number: 2011934524

Published by Cranberry Quill Publishing
111 Lamon Street, Suite 201
Fayetteville, NC 28301
www.CranberryQuill.com

First Edition

Printed in the United States of America

2 4 6 8 10 9 7 5 3 1

Edited by Jessica DeVault
Cover design by Keisha Clay
Photography by Dalton J. Carter
Layout by Sarah J. Hastings

Typeset in Times New Roman

Proverbs 31 (MSG)

A Hymn to a Good Wife

"A good woman is hard to find, and worth far more than diamonds. Her husband trusts her without reserve, and never has reason to regret it. Never spiteful, she treats him generously all her life long. She shops around for the best yarns and cottons, and enjoys knitting and sewing. She's like a trading ship that sails to faraway places and brings back exotic surprises. She's up before dawn, preparing breakfast for her family and organizing her day. She looks over a field and buys it, then, with money she's put aside, plants a garden. First thing in the morning, she dresses for work, rolls up her sleeves, eager to get started. She senses the worth of her work, is in no hurry to call it quits for the day. She's skilled in the crafts of home and hearth, diligent in homemaking. She's quick to assist anyone in need, reaches out to help the poor. She doesn't worry about her family when it snows; their winter clothes are all mended and ready to wear. She makes her own clothing, and dresses in colorful linens and silks. Her husband is greatly respected when he deliberates with the city fathers. She designs gowns and sells them, brings the sweaters she knits to the dress shops. Her clothes are well-made and elegant, and she always faces tomorrow with a smile. When she speaks she has something worthwhile to say, and she always says it kindly. She keeps an eye on everyone in her household, and keeps them all busy and productive. Her children respect and bless her; her husband joins in with words of praise: "Many women have done wonderful things, but you've outclassed them all!" Charm can mislead and beauty soon fades. The woman to be admired and praised is the woman who lives in the Fear-of-God. Give her everything she deserves! Festoon her life with praises!"

"But seek first his kingdom and his righteousness, and all these things will be given to you as well." **Matthew 6:33 (KJV)**

"Being confident of this very thing, that he which hath begun a good work in you will perform it until the day of Jesus Christ". **Philippians 1:6 (KJV)**

This poem was written by my friend and sister Carrie Elliott for her cousin Mertyse, the epitome of the Proverbs 31 woman.

31 Epitome: A Poem for Mertyse
By Carrie Elliott, PhD

She feared the Lord in all His glory, seeking His eternal grace;

Ever faithful and believing, she persevered and ran her race.

Though she carried her Cross, she gave us counsel; speaking life in every word;

Still she always paid heed to God's gentle voice – when He called her home she heard.

She smiled the sun's rays upon each of us, graciously embracing all of life's best.

Her soul-warming hugs said "you're in my heart", all who knew her can attest.

Her precious children rightly adored her, for she shared with them God's love;

What she wanted to give them while on this earth, she pours forth from heaven above.

Her hands were never idle, starting businesses – making plans;

She spoke with an eternal wisdom, holding to the Master's hand.

A passionate dreamer who saw no limits, what her mind conceived she did;

CEO of Inner Beauty Productions, modeling and etiquette she taught the kids.

Royal garments of strength and dignity she wore – beautiful from the inside out;

No matter the mountain, head toward the sky, never giving in to fear or doubt.

She encouraged us to see our own beauty, loving instructions rolled off her tongue;

While majestically and faithfully to the Father she climbed; rung by heavenly rung.

Now our angel is free of pain and suffering, homeward bound on the wings of a dove;

Her spirit will brightly shine forever, because she filled this world with love.

Today as we gather to celebrate Mertyse and reflect on her legacy;

She was a woman of righteousness; worth her weight in gold;

Our own Proverbs 31 Epitome

Table of Contents

Acknowledgements

This book would not have been possible without the grace and mercy of my Lord and Savior Jesus Christ. I thank the Holy Spirit for His help and comfort throughout this entire journey. I thank God for this life He has given me as well as the trials and tribulations He allowed to grow me up; and then bless me to bless others as a result through this book and through ministry.

I thank Him for loving His people so much that He would send me back to them with this Word and thereby bring them forth as well. I praise you God, and I thank you. You didn't have to do it, but I am SO glad that you did!

Dalton: The Bible says that, "He that findeth a wife findeth a good thing and obtaineth favor from the Lord." It doesn't mention how blessed a woman is when her husband finds her. I am truly blessed by God allowing you to find me. I love you more than you will ever know and I am so thankful for you and thankful that I get to take this journey and all of our life's journeys together with you - my best friend. You rock!

Miles: Thank you for letting me be your "other mom." I love you and I thank you for all of the lessons you have taught me, namely how to love unconditionally. I am getting there.

To my family: Daddy, Mommy, Michael, Garlinda, Marvin, Caleb and Miriam - thank you for always loving me and supporting me. We are a crazy, funny and amazing family and I thank God for placing me with all of you.

To my extended family: Mom and Dad Carter and Carla - thank you for accepting me into your family and into your hearts. I love you.

To all of my angels and sisterfriends: Bishop Veorah B. Davis, Dr. Johnie C. Davis, Elder Debbie G. Davis- thank you for helping me to walk in the beauty of holiness and the light of God. Pastor Kimberly Nixon, for helping me to find my way out, Kathy Frazier, Eileen Gilmore, Latascha Emanuel, Mona Hyppolite, Faith Thompson, Carrie Elliott, Sabrina Taylor, Dee Wells, Eileen Gilmore, Suzetta Perkins, Angela Tatum, Norma McLauchlin, Dina Lankford, Ben Simmons, Bill Snuggs and Zan Monroe, Carla Robinson and Stephanie L. Jones, Nancy Hightower and Jessica De Vault, Renee Gibbs and Belinda Guyton for your guidance and honesty. You each encouraged me, loved me, prodded me and threatened me to get this baby/book birthed. I thank you for being angels in human form.

To those who have gone on, especially Mae Forney and Edna Stewart and all of those who were so that we could be, I thank you.

x

Pray this prayer before you begin reading this book and before you begin your journey. We all need traveling mercies.

Heavenly Father, Abba, Daddy,

I come to you now to say thank you, to say I love you and to say, I bless Your name. It is my sincere desire to be the woman of God that you created and called me to be. I desire to change. Jesus, I accept you and recognize you now as my personal Lord and Savior. I repent of all of the words, thoughts; deeds and issues that I have that are contrary to who you are and who you would have me to be. Forgive me now, in your precious name.

Holy Spirit, I invite you in to be my guide and my comforter as I read, work, and live through this journey home. Through your help, I will be healed, delivered, set free and made whole, as God, my God intended, in Jesus' name!

Amen and thank YOU God!

Hallelujah~

Introduction

Why did I decide to write this book? Technically, I didn't decide, God did.

I speak to many women daily who are in unhappy, unfulfilled marriages with husbands and children, who they consider to be thankless. I speak to the single women, who believe God for a husband and who shake their heads at how remiss the married sisters are for lamenting over their husbands. For the singles sisters there are many lonely nights, tears and kisses from frogs who will never be princes and, well, you get the gist.

This book is for the women who strive to meet the standard of the godly woman in Proverbs 31.

Many books have been written about the Proverbs 31 woman, but I wanted to approach her from a different angle. I want to look at her as a *super* and *SUPERb* woman, and remind you of the super and superb woman you used to – or hope to – be. We all have this potential to be like this highly regarded woman of God. But somewhere along the way our inner *SUPERb* woman got lost.

This will serve as a testimony to those of us who desire greatness regardless of the battlefield raging in our flesh, our minds and our spirits in the forms of insecurity, broken-heartedness, and dreams deferred, single motherhood, diseases, and you name it. As *SUPERb* women, we owe it to every great-grandmother, grandmother, mother, aunt, sister, and girlfriend who has come before us and who planted the seeds of grace, strength, excellence and godliness within us to excel in the face of seemingly insurmountable odds. We owe it to them to forge ahead. Their legacy is now our legacy. If this is NOT the legacy you have been given, let it begin now with you.

We have all been through some things but in Christ, we are imbued with a power from on high. God has endowed us with a natural and supernatural ability to do all things through Him. – So why are we just getting by? Why are we settling for less? Why are our dreams bleeding and dying on the side of the road?

I really want to know what happened to YOU. Who came and ran you off your race?

Most importantly, *what are you going to do about it?!* If you're not sure, that's okay. I've come to help you find your way back home.

Where is home? Home is the place where God intended us to be all along. Home is where the Proverbs 31 woman met God. This is where she held His heart, while she let her light shine to the world around her, her family, her employees and her neighbors. Home is the place God intended us all to be and the place our spirit longs for.

Come, go with me.

* Please note that many chapters have journal entries for you to complete with as much thought as possible. Upon completion of this book, I would like for you to come back to each of your entries and see if your mindsets have changed.

The Original Bad Girl

Let's take a look back at the Proverbs 31 woman to examine who she was prior to her becoming the standard for godly women everywhere.

While birthing this book, I attended a writer's discussion where one of the authors suggested that we poll people to find out what they would like to know about our particular subject. Initially I was hesitant, but I felt the Holy Spirit saying, *do it.*

So, I sent an email to a number of sisterfriends asking them what their thoughts were regarding the Proverbs 31 woman and what they wanted to know about her. The responses were awesome and are shared at the end of this book.

My friend Eileen wrote back almost immediately with a hilarious response:

"First of all, whenever I read Proverbs 31, I am struck by the fact that I have no 'maidens' to help me at my house. Maybe that's how I can finally convince my husband to get a maid service - it's biblical!"

I'm not sure if this worked or not. I'll have to ask her.

However, it was what she went on to say that led me to dig deeper into who the Proverbs 31 woman actually was:

"It can, at first glance, seem that the Bible is setting up this unrealistic expectation of the perfect woman who finds a way to have it all [and be it all, who NEVER had drama and who is the epitome of perfection . . .Ugh!]. I also think the theories of biblical scholars are so interesting, too. Solomon is credited with writing much of Proverbs, as you know. But, chapter 31 states it was written by Lemuel, son of David and Bathsheba. It's supposed to be the teachings Bathsheba gave to Lemuel. She also is a living testimony to the fact that you can really screw up and that God not only loves you, but will work through you to make you a better person that before."

Do you know what this means? If Bathsheba was *the* Proverbs 31 woman, then that means:

1. We do not have to be perfect to come to God!

2. You can totally screw it up (as Eileen stated) and God will redeem you!

3. You may start out one way in your life, but that doesn't mean you have to stay that way!

4. We don't have to try and live up to this false expectation of perfection, rather, it's something we grow into as we continue to walk in the paths of righteousness that God has laid out for us!

Woohoo!!!!

My goal in this book is to help you return home. However, how can you return home if you don't first acknowledge where you came from?

Home for some may not be a place you want to return to; and ultimately, it is not the place I intend to take you; however, as we discussed previously, you MUST revisit the past so that you can move beyond it and on into the future.

As a means of doing this, I would like to look at Bathsheba's past; I will revisit my past too, and then we will go to your house. I say your house as in the present tense, because some of you are still *stuck* in the past and living it in the present.

Bathsheba's Business

Bathsheba was the daughter of Ammiel (also known as Eliam), a mighty man of David and a Levite tabernacle servant. He was also the son of Ahithophel, an advisor to David. In other words, she came from good, godly stock.

The name Bathsheba means, "Daughter of the Promise." The word "Bath" means daughter and "Sheba" means seven or to swear an oath. All together, her name means, "daughter of an oath" or "child of promise". This reminds me of the covenant that God made with Abraham regarding His blessings and the son he and Sarah would have -- even though they were past the age to conceive. An "oath" and a "promise" imply belief, reliance on God and patience. Patience is a virtue and one of the fruit of the Spirit[1]. Apparently, neither Bathsheba nor David embodied this virtue at our meeting them.

We meet Bathsheba, in 2 Samuel 11: 3. She is the wife of Uriah, a mighty man of valor in King David's army. She is beckoned by King David, sleeps with him and becomes pregnant thus causing her to become an adulteress. Subsequently, David has her husband killed and she goes on to become David's wife. I imagine this must have been as scandalous then as it is now. God spares David and Bathsheba but not the baby, who dies shortly after its birth. They come together again and end up giving birth to King Solomon. However, from the time of their sin, there is a curse of adversity on all of their future generations. Now this is definitely not the past you would consider for a woman who had descended from Levitican priests and men of valor, is it?

But wait; do we really have room to judge?

---

[1] Galatians 5:22-23

Are you acting in accordance to the teaching, upbringing and wisdom passed down throughout all these many generations of moms, aunties, grandmothers and even God himself?

Yes___ No___

Bathsheba's story is also a lesson in impatience and then patience, lust then holiness and so much more. Impatience can lead us down a path we never intended to walk and lead to forgetfulness - forgetfulness of who we are, forgetfulness of where we came from and forgetfulness and confusion of where we are going.

My story is not far off, with the exception of murder. God redeemed me from marital abuse, adultery, mental anguish, depression, an STD, defeat, low self-esteem, sexual sins and the list just goes on and on.

So, what does this mean? It means that we *all* have a past, that there is *nothing* new under the sun. More importantly, it means that God is a forgiving and redeeming God and that people CAN CHANGE if they want to. God can and will make our life brand new!

Bathsheba went *from* being a *bad girl to God's girl* and is now the epitome of what we all consider to be a *SUPERb Woman*.

Superb: Marked to the highest degree by grandeur, excellence, brilliance, or competence.

Do you know what this means? **We, too, can be SUPERb women of God!** So we know who Bathsheba was and who she became. Let's take a look at what you'll need for your trip.

SUPERb Woman Supply List

I was blessed to serve eight years in the United States Army Reserves. During that time, my unit never went on a journey or mission without receiving our orders and a supply list.

On your journey in life, you must receive orders and a supply list, too. Your orders come directly from God. He is the one with the plan and therefore, only He can tell you what the plan is. So ask Him.

"For I know the plans I have for you," declares the LORD, *"plans to prosper you and not to harm you, plans to give you hope and a future."* **Jeremiah 29:11 (NIV)**

Your supply list will include the following items:

A Uniform: The belt of truth; a breastplate of righteousness; shoes of readiness fitted for the gospel of peace; the shield of faith; the helmet of salvation and the sword of the Spirit, which is the word of God.

Food: Man shall not live by bread alone, but by every word that proceeds out of the mouth of God.

Shovel: Because you are going to have to dig your way out of some places.

A good attitude: Some of you are going to have trouble here because things will get tough.

Map: The steps of a good man are ordered by the Lord and He delighteth in his way.

Water: Jesus is the living water and the Holy Spirit is our help and comforter.

Prayer journal: Your prayer journal is located at the end of this book. You will need to read it daily as your daily bread for sustenance on this journey home.

Notebook: As you receive your orders, jot them down as they come, and take note of the pertinent facts, changes and occurrences.

Prepare to move out!

Check Your Map

Let's Begin YOUR journey home. The first thing you need to do is… check your map.

There were so many different directions and routes I could have taken as I was writing this book, so I diligently sought the Lord for His direction. Similarly, you have taken many different roadways at this point in your life and I venture to say that you may need to check your map.

I pray that you will take this the way Lord intends - wisely. Proverbs, as we know, is a book of wisdom and instruction. However, instructions only work if they are followed. In this chapter we will look to the map offered in Proverbs:

"If you love learning, you love the discipline that goes with it— how shortsighted to refuse correction! **"Proverbs 12:1 (MSG)**

Verse 28 continues, *"Good men and women travel right into life; sin's detours take you straight to hell."*

It is essential that you know which way and which direction you are going. The Word states that God will correct you if you do wrong or make a mistake. If you travel right, you will have life; whereas wrong decisions and detours will take you straight to hell.

So, have you checked your map? Which way are you going? Your path can be measured by lining your life up with the Word of God. If you're traveling the road of the righteous, you can expect to experience the fruit of the Spirit: love, joy, peace, patience, kindness, goodness, faithfulness, gentleness and self-control[2].

On the other hand, an unrighteous path yields fruit of the flesh like sexual immorality, impurity and debauchery; idolatry and witchcraft (characterized by a controlling, haughty, demeaning and/or demanding personality); hatred, discord, jealousy, fits of rage, selfish ambition, dissensions, factions and envy; drunkenness and orgies[3]. And since we are discussing modern day, let's add pornography, sexting, phone sex and the like. This roadmap leads to hell.

Get off this road now!

Once you have checked your map, you may realize that you took a few wrong turns. It's time now for a . . .

Redux: Also known as a redo or do-over; to be brought back, as in being reminded; formerly captive and now set free and allowed to return to one's true self, nature or home.

---

[2]Galatians 5:22-23
[3] Galatians 5:26

When looking back at your life, in hindsight, it's important to determine the source of your wrong turns. There are plenty of common reasons, one of them being distractions.

Distractions

It seemed impossible to write this book at times. When I wanted to write, there didn't seem to be a place conducive for writing. There didn't seem to be a 'quiet' place left in the world, including inside of my head. Even the coffee shops were a no-go. I was surrounded by noise, cigarettes (and no, I don't smoke) and people!

Argh!

But I was committed to birthing this Word as God had purposed it. I *must* write, yet it seemed to be one distraction after another. I had the burden, but then it ebbed, then it flowed. You may be able to relate, as many of you reading this have gotten off course multiple times as a result of distractions. Distractions can be allowed by God, sent by the devil in the form of snares, wrought from the noise and people who enter and remain in our life for far too long, and can be caused by decisions and actions we failed to pray and be led about prior to execution[4].

Praise God that He is a God of second chances. If you will just BE STILL[5], He will remove every distraction and place your feet back onto His intended and ordained path. Some of us have been on the path for so long we cannot even relate to anything else or may find it difficult to switch paths out of complacency or fear.

We simply MUST get focused!

Distractions can and have led to missed opportunities, aborted plans and a confusion of God's perfect will for our lives. They have led us from the path of righteousness directly into the wilderness, riddled with lions and tigers and *what is that*?! Once in the wilderness, we came under attack and ended up with unnecessary scars, wounds and heartache that feel as if they can take a lifetime to overcome. Even now, you may still be in an unhealed state, still distracted, still lost.

But according to Matthew 18:12, **God is here and He is saying, I have left the 99 to come after the one – YOU!**

---

[4]Romans 8:14; Isaiah 30:21.

[5]Psalm 46:10

Take a moment to complete the Journal Entry below. This step is important, because unless you acknowledge and examine the root of your distractions, you will continue to be hindered because of them.

What has caused you to become distracted?

expectations of other people
relying on myself instead of God

What are you willing to do to remove all of your distractions?

Do you want God to put you back on the path?

Prayer: *Father, in the name of Jesus Christ and by the power of the Holy Spirit, I ask you to remove all distractions **(name specifically)** and help me to see and hear Your voice. I declare that I will not lean to my own understanding, but I will acknowledge you in all my ways that you might direct my paths, according to your Word in Proverbs 3:5-6. Amen.*

Have You Seen Me?

Place a photo of yourself that represents who you were or who you want to be.

INSERT PHOTOGRAPH HERE

Accept Him

"Without God there is nothing, or without God 'no thing' matters…"

I can tell you from experience that one major problem exists and this is what has kept many from being able to get free: you don't have a relationship with Jesus Christ. Until you have accepted Him as your personal Lord and Savior; and made Him the head of your life, everything you do will be in vain, including the reading of this book. Choose to seek salvation NOW!

Salvation: Deliverance from the power and effects of sin.

My friend Carlie was a great inspiration for this chapter. She and I met over 20 years ago and she is just a beautiful, sweet and extremely energetic person. Carlie was also one of the first people my sister and I met when we arrived for our freshman year of college. We had lost touch since then. However, as many of us know, time passes and communication fades, but true friendship endures no matter what. When you pick up the phone or drop into each other's email boxes, it seems as if not even one moment has passed since you last spoke. Carlie and I have this type of friendship.

Fast forward 20 years to one month ago, when Carlie called me at seven o'clock in the morning stating that she needed to speak to me. I could hear from the sound of her voice that something was wrong. The bubbly effervescence she normally exuded was missing (unbeknownst to me, my husband said a silent prayer for her at that moment). I promised to call her as soon as I could pack my son into the car and drive him to school.

Once I completed my errand and picked up a much-needed cup of coffee at a local coffee shop, I called her. She began to tell me how tumultuous her life had been for the last year or so. And what a rollercoaster it had been! She was fired from her job after her employer became aware of her mental health diagnosis; she was in the middle of a lawsuit with said employer, too. There was also a recently divorced man who she really liked and was starting a business with. She was in therapy with a good therapist, filed bankruptcy and had moved in with her mother, all while striving to complete her Master's degree. She concluded her lengthy monologue by saying, "I know all of this would be better if my relationship with God was better."

"Well Carlie, speaking of which, how is your relationship with God," I asked.

She went on to tell me that she doesn't go to church like she should and neither does the young man of her interest. Well, while she was speaking, I could hear the Holy Spirit saying, *ask her about Jesus*. So I followed His lead and asked if she was saved.

"Well if you're asking me if I believe in God, yes, I do," she said.

I clarified, "More specifically, have you accepted Jesus as your personal Lord and Savior, according to Romans 10:9?"

She hadn't. From there, I shared with her that we could spend hours trying to go through and fix and discuss all of the issues she shared with me, but ultimately only Jesus could fix these things. In essence, with one prayer, He could begin the process of helping her sort all this out.

"I'm ready, but I need you to help me, because I'm not sure what to do," she replied enthusiastically. I prayed and asked the Holy Spirit to help me. We then opened our Bibles together and with her hundreds of miles away and me sitting in the parking lot at the coffee house, we read Romans 10:9 together. I told her that we should pray so that she could repent of her sins and invite Jesus to be Lord of her life.

Ain't God AMAZING?

Once we were finished, she said, "Patrice, tears are streaming down my face, and I just feel so much peace and so much better!"

God is *so* sweet that He can take all of our pain, despair, confusion, shame, fear, doubt, whatever and just wash it away and then rebuild us from scratch. I know the angels rejoiced for my friend that day, as they, too will rejoice for you[6].

God bless you and remember that you can focus on *a lot* of nothings and make them issues or problems. But they are really just distractions to keep you from accepting Jesus as your personal Lord and Savior and from knowing that God is able. Are you willing to look beyond your distractions to God? Without God no things and *nothing* matters.

If you are serious about wanting to be a Proverbs 31 woman, you *must* give your life to Christ. Take a moment to pray out loud the **Prayer of Salvation**[7]:

> *"God in Heaven, I come to you in the name of Jesus. I confess I have not lived my life for you. But I am glad to know I can change that. I have decided to accept that Jesus is your son, and that He died on the cross and rose again from the dead, so I might have eternal life and the blessings of life now. Jesus come into my heart, be my Savior, be my Lord. From this day forward and to the best of my ability, I will live my life for you. In Jesus' name, I pray. Amen."*

Congratulations on accepting Jesus Christ as your personal Lord and Savior!

"And I am certain that God, who began the good work within you, will continue his work until it is finally finished on the day when Christ Jesus returns." **Philippians 1:6 (NLT)**

Salvation Birth Date (*the date you received Jesus*): _____

---

[6] Luke 15:10
[7] Haley's Handbook

Who Were You?

For the next step in your journey, let's take a look back at you- the 'good' work He began. The purpose of going back is to get a clear picture of what you were like in the beginning, before…

It's funny because as I began to write this chapter, I had to reflect back to who I was. I remember being a shy, funny, very sweet person. I was a little girl, naïve, always dreaming, writing poetry; I was a book worm and a good friend. At least that's the me I saw.

Then as time went on, things changed. It was a long, painful trip home for me. But as a result, I have the ability to help you get home, too. So it was totally worth it.

Who do you remember yourself to be?

_____

_____

_____

_____

_____

_____

Some women will not want to look back on this reflection, but I urge you to do so. Until you look back and figure out who you were, you will never know who, what, when, where or why you are this person today. Good, bad or indifferent, God redeems ALL things. Look back, once more and prepare to move forward, because as Paul the Apostle said:

"Brethren, I count not myself to have apprehended: but this one thing I do, forgetting those things which are behind, and reaching forth unto those things which are before, I press toward the mark for the prize of the high calling of God in Christ Jesus!" **Philippians 3:13 (KJV)**

I know this may have been difficult for you and I can't say the remainder of the journey will be easier. However, I can tell you it will be worth it. Stick it out and let's move forward.

Hope Deferred…Dream Big

"Hope deferred makes the heart sick, but a longing fulfilled is a tree of life." **Proverbs 13:12 (NIV)**

Once upon a time, you dreamed of what your life would be like. You had plans for who you would be and what you would do. You may have wanted to be a model, a lawyer, an activist, an entrepreneur, a college graduate, an airline stewardess, and a missionary. Whatever you planned to be, I know it wasn't a doormat, a people pleaser, a drug addict, an alcoholic, a whore, or any of the other abominations we have been over time. Somewhere along the way, we fell into a pit.

Your Place

"And He said, hear now My words; if there is a prophet among you, I the Lord make Myself known to him in a vision and speak to him in a dream." **Numbers 12:6 (AMP)**

I share this because; God speaks to me in dreams and visions. Thus, I would like to share a dream with you He gave me one night. In the dream, I was in a wooded area. In the middle of a clearing in the woods, I saw a large muddy boiling area and a man walking about. The man was dressed like someone who was working and had on an apron. He looked weary and hot. Below the mud, I could see flames shooting up. As I continued to watch, people would walk into the mud and be sucked in. I asked the man, "Am I supposed to go in there?"

He said, ***"No, this place is not for you."***

When I woke up, I immediately began to seek God as to the meaning of this. The main thing that stood out to me was the miry clay. What in the world was this all about? I was led to search the Bible for any reference to the mud and the Word led me to **Psalm 40:2 (KJV)** that states:

"He also brought me up out of a horrible pit, out of the miry clay, and set my feet upon a rock, and established my steps."

I thought, okay this sounds like a good Word. The subtitle for this Psalm is, "Faith Persevering in Trial." As I began to study the reference scriptures, the Lord led me to, **Psalm 69:2 (KJV)** that states:

"I sink in deep mire, where *there is* no standing: I am come into deep waters, where the floods overflow me.."

Psalm 69:14 (WEB) continues:

"Deliver me out of the mire, and let me not sink; let me be delivered from those who hate me and out of the deep waters."

I came across my next reference in **Jeremiah 38:6** which shows the prophet Jeremiah speaking the Word of God to the people regarding their pending captivity and judgment. Some who heard the message disagreed, became angry and threw him into a pit. Jeremiah was later raised from the pit, as *this place was not for him.*

Next we are led to **Psalm 27:5 (KJV)**, one of my favorite Psalms and verses that states:

"For in the time of trouble He shall hide me in His pavilion; in the secret place of His tabernacle He shall hide me; He shall set me high upon a rock."

Okay, so it's all coming together, except I wanted to understand why Jeremiah was cast into the dungeon. Therefore, I went back to **Jeremiah 38:6** to search for answers - Stay with me, we're going somewhere.

The reason why Jeremiah was cast into the dungeon was for giving the Word of God that Jerusalem was to be taken captive by the Babylonians and that when the time came, everyone needed to surrender. God would save them as a result. God was allowing them to be taken into captivity as a result of their continued sin of idolatry and following the occults. Zedekiah was the king at that time and refused to receive the Word from the Prophet of the Lord, and refused to submit to the will of God.

Further, he spoke privately with Jeremiah to seek advice and shared his fears with the prophet. Jeremiah *implored* Zedekiah to allow himself and Jerusalem to be led into captivity and in doing so, God would preserve them and bring them out. If Zedekiah refused, Jeremiah shared with him the outcome, which would be the enslavement of Zedekiah's wife and children. Zedekiah would be seized and Jerusalem would be burned to the ground.

Zedekiah was afraid and refused to heed and believe the Word of God and therefore, brought destruction on himself and his family. And Jerusalem was still taken captive by the Babylonians. Keep in mind, Zedekiah's name was interpreted as "Righteousness of God." However, he was righteousness in name only. Righteousness is defined as doing what is morally right, genuine or good. Zedekiah refused to submit, therefore committing disobedience and unrighteousness.

THE POINT…

How many times in your life have you been faced with the Lord not being pleased with something or even someone in your life? Yet, you failed to listen or act by turning away out of fear or disobedience? Or, how many times has God given you a gift or a task to carry out and you have refused out of fear and disobedience?

As a result, you may have been led into a season where nothing you seemed to do worked and you felt boxed in or stuck in a situation. At this point, *many* people would begin to blame the devil or complain to God rather than to honestly search for the reason behind the situation – *themselves*. More than that, when God does identify us as the problem, we often turn away and say, "No Lord, it's not me!"

There are many lessons in this chapter. I will state them simply so that you can apply them to your life, as led by the Lord:

Lesson One: Be Bold

If God has given you *something* to do or say, then you know there is a mandate from God on your life. You need to get to it and stop being afraid. Jeremiah was called at a young age by God. When God commissioned him, He told Jeremiah, *"Get yourself ready! Stand up and say to them whatever I command you. Do not be terrified by them, or I will terrify you before them.* 18Today I have made you a fortified city, an iron pillar and a bronze wall to stand against the whole land—against the kings of Judah, its officials, its priests and the people of the land. 19They will fight against you but will not overcome you, for I am with you and will rescue you,"* declares the LORD. **"Jeremiah 1: 17-19** (NIV)

Hence, **Psalm 27:5**; God will hide you! **BE BOLD!**

Lesson Two: Don't Fear Captivity

God led Jerusalem into captivity for a purpose. His reason was to lead them into captivity as a result of their continued sin and to show them His loving kindness and tender mercy. This doesn't make Him a mean God, it makes Him a *just* God. He has to punish sin because there is *no* sin in Him. He cannot allow or approve of sin in us. His Word says that He will punish sin, so if He doesn't, it would make Him a liar and immoral. However, we can see that God is still a gracious and loving God. He tells Jerusalem and Zedekiah to submit to this captivity and He will keep them in the midst of it and He will bring them out of it.

Some of us are in captivity right now - a relationship, a job, financially, mentally, emotionally or even spiritually. Are you fighting in the midst of it to get out or are you seeking God to find out why you're in it and what you need to learn or do while you're there? He has already promised to keep you and to bring you out.

Lesson Three: Make a Choice

I want to remind you about the dream I shared. When I asked the man about the mire, he said to me, *"This place is not for you."* Remember, Jeremiah was lowered into the mire, but he was raised out of it, because God promised to deliver Him for doing His will. And because Jeremiah obeyed God that pit and place was not for him either.

So I ask, is this place for you?

The answer is either 'yes' or 'no', depending on how you proceed. If you desire to continue on the way you are going, taking your own way, living according to your own reasoning, sinning and operating in fear or choosing to please people over God, *this place is likely for you.* However, if you decide to turn away right now, repent and make a stand for righteousness and trust God, you will be released from captivity and *this place will not be for you.*

Zedekiah had a choice, Jerusalem had a choice and now you have to decide.

Is this place for me? God has promised deliverance and He is just and able to perform it, but the first step is ours to make. Please choose wisely and be blessed.

What were your dreams?

_____

_____

_____

Who did you want to become?

_____

_____

_____

When did you become sidetracked?

_____

_____

_____

Who or what caused you to be sidetracked?

_____

_____

_____

What are your dreams now?

_____

_____

_____

Who do you now desire to be?

_____

_____

_____

What can you do RIGHT NOW to get back on track?

_____

_____

_____

Do you know that it's NEVER too late, according to Isaiah 43:18-25?

_____

Starting Over

There may be some places in your life, where you simply need to start over. I remember that at the same time I met my husband, God was telling me to cut off my fake nails and all of my relaxed hair off. There were also clothes I did not need to wear any longer; they were not part of my destiny. In other words, they didn't need to be packed for the next leg of my journey.

I realized that God had done the work of changing me on the inside and now, He wanted to make over my outside. There was nothing wrong with the way I looked. I simply needed to leave that part of who I was in the past with everything else and go forward as a completely "new" creature.

"Therefore, if anyone is in Christ, he is a new creation; the old has gone, the new has come!" **2 Corinthians 5:17 (NIV)**

I remember thinking, "Lord, all of my hair is gone! What is my husband going to think now when he sees me?" I was thinking about the outer man, but it was the inner man - my inner beauty - that God was perfecting and this is what my husband saw. Thank the Lord, because that new outer look could have gone really wrong! (Just kidding!)

Charm is deceptive, and beauty is fleeting; but a woman who fears the LORD is to be praised. **_(Proverbs 31:30) (NIV)_**

My point here is that– in terms of your life–it is never too late to start over. Let the Lord lead you into this truth. It was inspiring to me that Bathsheba started over after David killed her husband so they could be together. She lost her baby as a result of this sin. Yet, God still redeemed her life and helped her to become a woman who was held in high esteem, as the Proverbs 31 woman, even to this day.

Why can't you do the same? Make the choice to start over right now.

Where do you need to start?

_____

_____

_____

_____

_____

_____

So far, we have spent time delving into ourselves - past and present. We will get to the future -you- eventually. However, the next part of our journey involves an examination of us as a Proverbs 31 wife and a Proverbs 31 single woman. Each season – single and married – is a ministry unto God.

As a single woman, you are married to God until the time He presents you to your husband. And as a married woman, you are married to your husband, whose responsibility is to seek God for help in leading your family. Each ministry is a testimony to our love of God. As believers, God refers to us as His betrothed and He is our bridegroom. Therefore, we are consistently in a state of marriage and ministry.

When the Bible first introduced us to Bathsheba, she was married. Given this, we will take a moment now to delve into marriage as a ministry and work towards becoming the Proverbs 31 wife God intended us to be.

Come go with me.

Marriage Ministry

REBELLION
BITTERNESS
ADULTERY
GREED
INDECISION
CONDEMNATION
LUST

Which Wife Are You?

I recently met with a 'friend' of mine who needed someone to talk to. She needed a listening ear and, I believe, an understanding of her situation. I laughingly shared with her that I'd just labored through a similar situation and was sent of God to help her through her delivery. Her dilemma and our ensuing discussion centered on her experience as a wife and the struggle she was currently having with her spouse.

While driving home, from our meeting, the Holy Spirit gave me this topic: *What wife are you?*

Proverbs 31:10 (NKJV) states: *"Who can find a virtuous wife? For her worth is far above rubies."*

Virtuous: Moral, righteous, ethical, noble, potent, powerful, effective.

So this virtuous woman is excellent in character. There are *many* types of wives mentioned throughout the Bible. Sift through your spirit to see if you can identify with any of them:

Mary: Holy and submitted to God.

Elizabeth: A good friend and Christian.

Jezebel: Manipulative and controlling. She would do *anything* to get what she wanted.

Sarah: A sister-friend, loving and loyal wife to Abraham; barren.

Eve: Negatively influential; given to distraction and misinformed.

Lot's wife: Stuck in the past and unwilling to change.

Rebekah: Played favorites with her children and kept secrets from her husband.

Ruth: A wise and loving wife with a teachable and humble spirit.

Michal: Jealous, bitter and disrespectful.

Esther: Beautiful and courageous.

Job's Wife: Lacking in faith and unsupportive.

Gomer: Adulterous.

Delilah: Nagging, malicious and untrustworthy.

Sapphira: Greedy and deceptive.

Priscilla: A partner in every sense of the word; hardworking.

Take a moment to meditate and pray: *"Holy Spirit, please reveal to me what type of wife I am, in Jesus' name."*

Be still and hear Him.

Write what you hear or what you may already know about the type of wife you are:

_____

_____

_____

Is this the wife you want to be? Yes___ No___

If not, then what are you going to do about it?

_____

_____

_____

What type of wife would you like to be?

_____

If you cannot answer or identify with more than one wife (in a not so good way) repent to God and your husband. Ask the Holy Spirit to help you become the wife God intended you to be. Also, speak to your pastor and study the Word of God.

PRAYER: Father in the name of Jesus, help me, through the power of the Holy Spirit, to become the godly wife you created and intended me to be. Amen.

And remember: _"The wise woman builds her house, but with her own hands the foolish one tears hers down."_ **Proverbs 14:1 (NIV)**

My Man, Your Man, You

"Her husband is greatly respected when he deliberates with the city fathers." **Proverbs 31:23 (MSG)**

A huge part of Proverbs 31 is spent discussing _all_ of the many things the virtuous woman did: cooking, cleaning, mending, owning a business, buying real estate, managing her household staff, raising her children. But I _always_ wondered, "Well, what was 'her man' doing while she was doing all of these things? And, how did she feel about it?"

Essentially, she was - and we are - **Helpmates or Helpmeets**. The Merriam-Webster Dictionary defines this term as "**a wife.**"

Do you see yourself as a helpmeet, a wife? Or does the mere mention of that term make you uncomfortable?

_____

_____

My husband and I have a couples Bible study that we purchased before we married. As we go through the studies, we have lengthy discussions about particular chapters in the book. One of the chapters was about Ahab and Jezebel and Adam and Eve.

We discussed how a husband could be away at times or out of place in terms of his place in the family structure, according to God's standard. In regards to this, we talked about how Eve fed Adam the apple and how Jezebel just – to put it nicely - henpecked Ahab to death. Essentially, each one deceived her husband in some way but in Proverbs 31, we see that her husband is respected and that he considers his wife to be a jewel. He trusts her.

How does your man see you? Can he trust you? If not, why?

_____

_____

_____

_____

"*In a marriage relationship, there is authority from Christ to husband, and from husband to wife. The authority of Christ is the authority of God. Any man, who speaks with God or about God in a way that shows a lack of respect for the authority of Christ, dishonors Christ. In the same way, a wife who speaks with God in a way that shows a lack of respect for the authority of her husband dishonors her husband. Worse, she dishonors herself—an ugly sight, like a woman with her head shaved. This is basically the origin of these customs we have of women wearing head coverings in worship, while men take their hats off. By these symbolic acts, men and women, who far too often butt heads with each other, submit their 'heads' to the Head: God.*"
1 Corinthians 11:3-9 (MSG)

Many women discount their husband's role and importance in their life and this is a *critical and crucial error* spiritually and in every other way. Why? Because all things begin and end with God.

30

*"I am **Alpha** and **Omega**, the beginning and the ending, saith the Lord, which is, and which was, and which is to come, the Almighty."* **Revelation 1:8 (KJV)**

In essence, if you discount, discard, disrespect, and cause harm to your husband in anyway, *YOU* are out of the will and covering of God. As much as many women don't believe it or accept it, you – I and we – *need* our husbands.

Repeat these words: "I need my husband and my husband needs me!"

In this section, I was moved to write about the husband as our "covering" and the "order" of marriage. There are *so* many couples we have met recently that are out of order in different ways. I have met a number of wives who have been called to the ministry by God, but because of their husband's state of unreadiness, the woman will not move out and do the will of God. I have also met other wives who have ventured into new business opportunities (i.e. quitting their job) without the approval or consent of their husbands, because God told them to do so. Lastly, I have met women who are operating in their God-given calling, but completely disrespect and disregard their husbands, because he is not operating in his calling.

Wow!

Well, what does God say about it? Let's go to the Word of God and then tie it all together:

"Husbands, love your wives, as Christ loved the church and gave Himself up for her." **Ephesians 5:25 (ESV)**

"Husbands, love your wives [be affectionate and sympathetic with them] and do not be harsh or bitter or resentful toward them." **Colossians 3:19 (AMP)**

"However, let each man of you [without exception] love his wife as (being in a sense) his very own self; and let the wife see that she respects and reverences her husband (that she notices him, regards him, honors him, prefers him, venerates, and esteems him; and that she defers to him, praises him, and loves and admires him exceedingly)." **Ephesians 5:33 (AMP)**
For further clarification, read 1 Peter 3:2.

Your husband must love you enough to respect, listen to and consider your feelings, needs, wants, and desires.

We must obtain favor, love and respect from our husbands, as we have given to them, as Queen Esther did[8]. And we must trust God to move on our husband's heart and at times move forward regardless of the consequences. The "but" is we *must* let LOVE guide all of our actions[9].

Prayer: *Father, in the name of Jesus and through the power of the Holy Spirit, please forgive me for where I have fallen short as a helpmeet in not respecting my husband, by complaining against him and complaining against You, God. I ask that you will restore to me the joy of your salvation and that you would give me favor with my husband and a renewed strength and energy to be the wife you intended me to be. Amen.*

I Got Him, Now What?

I don't know about you, but we can all relate to a time when we brought our "A" game while being courted by our spouse. I mean, everything was waxed, primped, primed and plumped. There was NO "half- steppin'" in the area of clothing, makeup, hair, perfume, jewelry, shaving, etc. *Then,* we got married and for some of us, including me, the little red wagon just took a turn and laid over on the side of the road.

We stopped shaving, pulled the 'doo-rag' back out, and pulled out the nappy sweat pants with the paint spots. And *Oh Lord,* out came the fuzzy socks! I bet our husbands were thinking, "The devil is a LIAR!"

I fell short and had to regroup, redirect and rearrange some things, such as revisiting my "flyness," so that "Mister" could remember what attracted him to me in the first place and to also keep him on his toes, if you know what I mean. I read an article - thank you, Holy Spirit - written in our local paper from a husband who wanted advice. From that point, I knew I had to get some things straight.

The article read, "My wife and I have been together for eight years and she is a good person. However, she is needy and needs constant assurance that I am attracted to her," his letter to the columnist began.

He continues to state that he is struggling to maintain his attraction to his wife because, "She uses the bathroom - numbers 1 and 2 - with the door open; she has skin issues and makes them worse by coming to bed with the acne med or open sores; and she passes gas often and loud in front of me."

---

[8] Esther 5
[9] Galatians 5:33

Further, he goes on to state that she is constantly wearing these nasty sweatpants and her hair is a mess. You couldn't make this stuff up! Her girlfriends, according to hubby, are "cut from the same cloth", and therefore they all think it's the husband who has the issue.

My point, in case you're still not getting it, is this: You need to do the same things now that you did before you were married (i.e. keep up your self-maintenance). Men tend to not want to get into discussions with us surrounding whether or not we look fat in this dress. Have I put on weight? Do you still find me attractive? Why don't you come on to me anymore?

Beloved, if we have to ask this or any other related questions, we already know the answer and we need to get it together.

I got the message. I invested in some new makeup and took the time to look cute. And I threw out my old nasty sweats (guilty as charged). There are some other areas I need to and will improve on, in Jesus' name.

This is not intended to sound shallow or make you feel bad. But we must understand that men are visual. If makeup is not your thing, or you are cool with your weight, clothing, etc., it's okay. All I am advocating is consistency in looking good, smelling good and being good for your husband in the way that he wants.

If you don't believe that men are visual or don't pay attention, read the Song of Solomon, in the Bible. Solomon didn't miss any details, and the Shulamite woman definitely caught his eye. Our girl, Proverbs 31 was no slacker either. So we don't have any excuses!

Is your husband saying these types of things to you?:

"You're so beautiful, my darling, so beautiful, and your dove eyes are veiled. By your hair as it flows and shimmers, like a flock of goats in the distance streaming down a hillside in the sunshine. Your smile is generous and full - expressive and strong and clean. Your lips are jewel red, your mouth elegant and inviting, your veiled cheeks soft and radiant. The smooth, lithe lines of your neck command notice—all heads turn in awe and admiration! Your breasts are like fawns, twins of a gazelle, grazing among the first spring flowers. The sweet, fragrant curves of your body, the soft, spiced contours of your flesh. Invite me, and I come. I stay until dawn breathes its light and night slips away. You're beautiful from head to toe, my dear love, beautiful beyond compare, absolutely flawless. **"Song of Solomon 4:1-7 (MSG)**

Or….

"Come with me from Lebanon, my bride. Leave Lebanon behind, and come. Leave your high mountain hideaway. Abandon your wilderness seclusion, where you keep company with lions and panthers guard your safety. You've captured my heart, dear friend. You looked at me,

and I fell in love. One look my way and I was hopelessly in love! How beautiful your love, dear, dear friend - far more pleasing than a fine, rare wine, your fragrance more exotic than select spices. The kisses of your lips are honey, my love, every syllable you speak a delicacy to savor. Your clothes smell like the wild outdoors, the ozone scent of high mountains. Dear lover and friend, you're a secret garden, a private and pure fountain. Body and soul, you are paradise,

a whole orchard of succulent fruits - Ripe apricots and peaches, oranges and pears; nut trees and cinnamon, and all scented woods; mint and lavender, and all herbs aromatic; a garden fountain, sparkling and splashing, fed by spring waters from the Lebanon mountains." Song of **Solomon 4:8-15 (MSG)**

If not, you might want to get to work, sis!

Let the Marriage Bed Be Undefiled

Prior to getting married, my husband and I sought pre-marital counseling from each of our respective pastors. Some of the advice they gave us was: 1.Don't go to bed angry, 2.Try to not get angry at the same time; and, 3.Walk in agreement, forgive and be sure to maintain intimacy.

1 Corinthians 7:3-5 (NIV) tells us this:

"The husband should fulfill his marital duty to his wife, and likewise the wife to her husband. The wife's body does not belong to her alone but also to her husband. In the same way, the husband's body does not belong to him alone but also to his wife. Do not deprive each other except by mutual consent and for a time, so that you may devote yourselves to prayer. Then come together again so that Satan will not tempt you because of your lack of self-control."

Well, about three months into our marriage, we were visiting with our Pastor and he asked how we were doing. We both said, "Fine."

He then asked, "How's your sex life?"

O-M-G! I was *so* mortified! We both fell out laughing and we said, "You know, everything is working out fine, thank you for asking!"

Needless to say, my husband and I were both thinking, *"Awkward!"*

However, the Holy Spirit reminded me of this as I sat down to complete this chapter. There are *numerous* couples, many of them Christian, who have not had sex with each other in days, weeks, months maybe even years. I know, because I have been friends with some of them and prayed with others concerning this very issue.

If you are married and you are not having sex, that is a problem. There are numerous reasons why couples suffer in their sexual intimacy. I was reminded of a few and will share them:

- Unforgiveness
- Bitterness
- Adultery
- Domestic Control
- Loss of interest
- Medical condition
- Lack of agreement
- Lack of understanding

I challenge you to determine why you and your spouse may be struggling in this area. While we were dating, my husband and I watched a teaching series on issues we should be in total agreement on prior to getting married. One of those areas was sexual intimacy.

Questions we were to discuss were how often we'd be intimate, our likes and dislikes, our deal breakers and things of that nature. Please note we were in agreement that we would abstain from sex until we were married. Therefore, this conversation was held in a neutral setting without explicit detailing and lasted long enough for us to get an understanding and an agreement and be done.

In terms of premarital counseling, I don't know if couples have done this or do this prior to marriage; however, I believe it is very beneficial, as it will lead to an open dialogue and understanding so that any issues can be worked out beforehand. If you are already married it is not too late to sit down with your spouse now and get it straight.

There is power in agreement. The Word of God tells us: *"Again, I tell you that if two of you on earth agree about anything you ask for, it will be done for you by my Father in heaven."* **Matthew 18:19 (NIV)**

He said, "ANYTHING!"

If you are experiencing this issue in your marriage, help is available. My suggestion would be to discuss any areas of sexual unfulfillment with your spouse first. Pray together and seek God, especially in those areas where you are not in agreement. Please **<u>DO NOT</u>** seek advice from ungodly or unsaved married or single friends, outside acquaintances or family. The Bible tells us there is safety in a multitude of counselors. However, we must ask God who He would have us to speak to.

If you and your spouse fail to find resolution, seek assistance from your pastor, a respected counselor, books and even a medical professional. Your marriage is worth it, but you have to be in agreement.

Side Note: For the spouse who may not want to seek counseling, because you don't want people in your business, this is an excuse - a poor one at that. This stems from pride. Is this worth losing your marriage over?

Many seek out affairs, alcohol, drugs, pornography and other forms of idolatry as a means of coping. But these will only further defile you and undermine the foundation and covenant on which your marriage was established. I know from personal experience.

It is simply NOT worth it.

Lastly, a lack of understanding is a HUGE issue in many marriages. The Bible tells us: *"Do two walk together unless they have agreed to do so?* **Amos 3:3 (NIV)**

The word "agreement" is synonymous with "understanding."

> **Understanding:** A friendly or harmonious relationship; an agreement of opinion or feeling; adjustment of differences.

What do you and your spouse need to get into agreement and understanding about?

_____

_____

_____

_____.

This Word is for husbands and wives. In regards as to why intimacy and sex may suffer in a marriage, I feel it is vitally important for you and your spouse to uncover those reasons and begin to deal with these issues. God ordained and created marriage to be beautiful, productive, intimate, and multiple other adjectives. Marriage is so important that He refers to us as His Beloved and His Bride. He is doing and will do everything possible to make our relationship with Him work, to include sacrificing His only son Jesus, on our behalf[10].

---

[10] John 3:16

What are you willing to sacrifice to turn this area of your life around?

_____

_____

_____

Adultery

"Your spring water is for you and you only, not to be passed around among strangers. Bless your fresh-flowing fountain! Enjoy the wife you married as a young man! Lovely as an angel, beautiful as a rose— don't ever quit taking delight in her body. Never take her love for granted! Why would you trade enduring intimacies for cheap thrills with a whore? For dalliance with a promiscuous stranger?" **Proverbs 5:17-20 (MSG)**

I remember when God first gave me the vision to write this book, a friend of mine said to me, "When you write, don't try and play it safe. Write from your heart and be 'real' with people. Give them the good, the bad and the ugly."

I guess this section qualifies as the bad and the ugly. The good is in the end, so hang on with me. I want to tell my story in a way that brings honor to God, doesn't offend or misrepresent my ex-husband and will help you in some way.

Help me Holy Spirit.

I shared this with my awesome, God-given husband and he is okay with me sharing. I was married for the first time in 1996, and at the time, I was 28, unsaved, immature and just coming out of a seven-year relationship. I met my ex-husband in a club through a mutual friend. What attracted me to him were his looks. He was really handsome and extremely confident. The first thing I said to him was, "Do you want to go down to South Carolina tonight and get married?"

I just knew I'd found my husband! I had not based this assumption on anything other than the fact that he was good-looking. I know, it sounds so pathetic just writing it. At the time of our meeting, my ex-husband was separated, but not divorced from his second wife and even tackier to say, I found and drove him to the attorney's office so that he could file his divorce and be free to be with me.

The revelation I had as I was writing this passage is that I was already committing adultery even before we were married. And our marriage was based on physicality and lots of emotion. I have since repented.

Like many women, I ignored multiple signs that I was off course to include:

- Neither of us was saved
- We had no premarital counseling
- I pursued him
- I committed adultery with him, as he was not divorced
- I moved in with him after only knowing him for a short period of time
- I was still unhealed from the previous relationship
- I had ALWAYS been in relationships. I couldn't remember EVER not being in a relationship
- We fought often, and it was increasingly dramatic and at times violent (i.e. throwing stuff, holes being punched in the walls, verbal abuse, dishes being broken, and threats on my life)
- I worshiped the ground he walked on
- I was a chronic people pleaser
- I had low self-esteem
- I saw the signs of things to come but I felt like I could handle it

There is more, but I think you get the picture.

In 1996, we were married and I was completely into being married to him. I thought the sun rose and set with him. He, on the other hand, liked being married when it fit in with what he had going on. We were constantly at odds about the lack of 'quality' time he spent with me and the lack of affection he would show. I spent a lot of time alone and would even go out alone. He was always, even from the beginning, accusing me of "messing around" and was very suspicious and jealous of my past friendships. He was wrong. I was not messing around with anyone. We lived in my hometown, so I knew many people and was friendly with everyone. I am a hugger and here in the South, hugs are just part of what we do.

I was faithful and committed regardless of what he thought until about the fifth year of our marriage. By this time, I was completely depressed, lonely, still battling the aforementioned issues and was going out pretty often and drinking as often as I could. As you can imagine, I left myself open to multiple opportunities to meet other men and one sin led to another.

In the last year of our marriage, I had actually accepted Jesus as my Lord and Savior, but was not clear on what this actually meant. Hence, I lived with one foot in the church and one foot in the world. To say the least, I was tormented. In the midst of this, I became pregnant and I

38

didn't know to whom the baby belonged. At this point, I knew (as my sister had warned), God had taken His hand completely off me. He allowed me to escape the situation only with my life. I had a tubal pregnancy and lost the baby and the tube.

Shortly thereafter, my marriage ended. He left me. He left because the Lord made me tell him the truth. I'd had multiple affairs and had lied to him about them. I also had to tell my family and my friends the awful truth about the life I had led. I considered suicide but the Lord said, "No." In the end, I had to take a *long* journey, and it began with the truth.

The truth was ***I was a mess.*** There are no other excuses to be made or blame to be placed as each action I took came from a decision that I consciously made. If this is a situation that you find yourself in, please stop and take a moment to ***admit your mess***, because otherwise, you are not going to be able to move forward.

The next thing the Lord did was reveal to me the way He viewed me in light of the way I had lived my life up to this point and, it wasn't pretty. It was HARD to hear, but the Word of God says: *"Then you will know the truth, and the truth will set you free."* **John 8:32 (NIV)**

The Word the Lord shared with me about myself came out of **Proverbs 7:6-27**. Needless to say, this was a jagged, bitter pill to swallow. It hurt so bad to hear the Lord refer to me in this way. And more than that, it was terrifying to think that I was headed to hell and taking other people with me.

In case you don't read it, the characteristics of the woman God is referring to in **Proverbs 7:6-27** are:

- DECEPTIVE
- BRAZEN
- RESTLESS
- SEDUCING
- ROAMING (NEVER AT HOME)
- WHORISH, ON THE WAY TO THE GRAVE
- SINFUL
- CONNIVING
- REBELLIOUS
- DRESSED LIKE A PROSTITUTE (SHOWING EVERYTHING)
- PERSUASIVE

It was all true and it was all me and all I could do was cry and repent and cry some more for the mess that I had made of everything. I went through this period of depression and guilt. I was unable to forgive myself and was just sick for the pain I had caused my husband and for the pain I had caused God and the mess I had made of my life to this point.

But, one thing about God, He IS a God of second chances. Once I repented and submitted to the process of allowing God to clean me up and clean me out, He began to reveal to me the woman that He had originally intended me to be prior to my veering off course.

He gave me forgiveness, grace, mercy, independence, education, and multiple work opportunities. Then five years later, He gave me the love of my life, my best friend and a son to go along with it - all on the same day.

This journey is one that is ongoing. However, I now know why the enemy fights us even before we can get to God. He, too, knows who God has intended us to be - or he at least has some idea - and his job is to abort that plan. We assist in this by taking the path of sin and making our own choices as opposed to yielding to God and letting Him direct our path.

If you are a spouse who is considering an affair or who has committed adultery, please read **Proverbs 7:6-27** and know that your sins are *not* hidden from God and they will find you out. There is a better way.

Furthermore, if you have committed these acts and are no longer doing so, but find yourself stuck in a state of unforgiveness and depression, please know that God forgives all things if we repent and turn away.

"If we confess our sins, he is faithful and just and will forgive us our sins and purify us from all unrighteousness." **1 John 1:9 (NIV)**

And **Romans 8:1 (NIV)** tells us, *"Therefore, there is now no condemnation for those who are in Christ Jesus."*

Make it a point, RIGHT NOW, to stop what you are doing or planning to do. Know what God's thoughts are on adultery, seek counseling with or without your spouse and decide that you will choose to honor your marriage covenant with God in your relationship to Him, your spouse and within your own body.

Use the Proverbs 31 woman as your guide: Proverbs 31:12; 31: 27 (NIV) she brings him good not harm, all the days of her life. She watches over the affairs of her household and does not eat the bread of idleness.

Domestic Control

I debated, off and on, whether to include this chapter or not. I feel as though the Lord would have me to so, here we are.

Domestic control is defined, by my experience, as living in a house where there is a dominant spirit of control, and as such, we are not able to fully be yourself. This is so, because the other person wants desperately for you to act and be the way they want you to.
This, is not the will of God.

Now, I know that we have briefly touched on this in multiple chapters, however, this situation is slightly different. This is written for those of you who are: 1. In a relationship (not married), 2. Shacking (i.e. living together) or married, and your significant other is so controlling to the point, that your nerves are constantly on edge, you feel sick to your stomach, you live in fear, but you just love them so much and believe they can change. I know this sounds wordy and chaotic, but then so is your situation.

My response here is multi-fold:

- If you are in a non-married relationship and there are no children involved- RUN FOR YOUR LIFE AND DON'T LOOK BACK. You have permission to do so.

- If you are in a non-married relationship and there are children involved- RUN FOR YOUR LIFE AND DON'T LOOK BACK. You have permission to do so.

- If you are married and may or may not have children, YOU MUST GET HELP. I say this because a controlling situation has many faces, there may be verbal abuse, mental and emotional abuse, physical abuse, and in some instances all three. YOU MUST GET HELP.

- Talk to your family and friends.

- Speak to your Pastor.

- Find a shelter for victims of domestic violence.

God is able to do all things, but fail; however, it is His desire that His children be free. He has not called us to live under the negative control of anyone or anything.

"Don't you realize that this is not the way to live? Unjust people who don't care about God will not be joining in his kingdom. Those who use and abuse each other, use and abuse sex, use and abuse the earth and everything in it, don't qualify as citizens in God's kingdom. A number of you know from experience what I'm talking about, for not so long ago you were on that list. Since then, you've been cleaned up and given a fresh start by Jesus, our Master, our Messiah, and by our God present in us, the Spirit." **1 Corinthians 6:9 (MSG)**

Abuse, which is a form of control, is not the will of God for your life. I dealt with verbal, mental and emotional abuse for years, and I died a slow death, EVERY DAY. Eventually it became physical; however, God removed me before it became as bad as it could have been.

Part of what kept me there was I could not believe that as an educated, well-raised woman, I was allowing myself to accept such treatment and I kept up the erroneous belief that one day things would magically change. They never did.

I am pleading with you; please take a stand for yourself, and for your children. I did and I know and believe that you can too.

Unforgiveness, Bitterness and Loss of Interest

I heard the Holy Spirit say; *"Your relationship with your spouse reflects your relationship with God."*

What does this mean for you? For some the answer will be a hearty, "Amen." For others of you reading this, you might say, "Ouch!"

Previously, we discussed marriage and adultery. I felt it necessary to tie in three areas that can truly wreak havoc on a marriage: Unforgiveness, bitterness and loss of interest.

Unforgiveness: A state of having or making no allowance for error or weakness.

Where would we be if God had not sacrificed Jesus for us, and if He had been unforgiving and made no way of escape or atonement for us?

Matthew 6:14-15 (NIV) tells us God's thoughts on forgiveness: *"For if you forgive other people when they sin against you, your heavenly Father will also forgive you. But if you do not forgive others their sins, your Father will not forgive your sins."*

The other part of the whole unforgiveness thing is you act as though you have never been wrong! Or that the other person's wrong is so much greater than yours. Says who?

Moving on…

Unforgiveness leads to bitterness. This happens because as those toxic emotions settle in and fester within your spirit man, a root begins to form and it permeates your entire existence. You begin to speak and act differently and soon everyone is able to take part in the putrid state of your heart.

Unforgiveness is a sin and the root of bitterness is its offspring.

Stop and pray right now: *"Father God, please help me, through the power of the Holy Spirit, to begin to forgive, and, I ask that You please remove the root of bitterness that has sprung up in my heart. Restore to me the joy of Your salvation and uphold me by Your right hand. Give me peace, in Jesus' name. Amen."*

The last area for us to discuss here is, **lack of interest**. A lack of interest can occur in a marriage for a number of reasons, to include, work, children, exhaustion, unforgiveness, boredom, busyness, etc. Regardless of the reason, this needs to be addressed immediately.

1 Corinthians 7:1-7 (NIV) tells us*: "Now for the matters you wrote about: 'It is good for a man not to have sexual relations with a woman. But since sexual immorality is occurring, each man should have sexual relations with his own wife, and each woman with her own husband. The husband should fulfill his marital duty to his wife, and likewise the wife to her husband. The wife does not have authority over her own body but yields it to her husband. In the same way, the husband does not have authority over his own body but yields it to his wife. Do not deprive each other except perhaps by mutual consent and for a time, so that you may devote yourselves to prayer. Then come together again so that Satan will not tempt you because of your lack of self-control. I say this as a concession, not as a command. I wish that all of you were as I am. But each of you has your own gift from God; one has this gift, another has that."*

The point here is that when we abstain from sexual intimacy with our mate for too long, we allow the enemy a foothold through which to enter our marriage. The sexual union strengthens your marriage bonds, to your spouse and to God. He tells us in His Word, "A threefold cord is not easily broken[11].

It takes two to do this, but only one person to initiate it. You be the one. Yes, I know that you may always be the one initiating everything. That is not the point. As you operate in love and obedience, God will see to it that your spouse does so as well.

---

[11] Ecclesiastes 4:12

What can you do right now to restore your connection with your spouse and regain your passion and interest for one another? Take the first step.

_____

_____

_____

_____

Commit to doing it NOW and continuing to do it - consistently. Remember that God is in this marriage with us. Our relationship with our spouse reflects our relationship with Him.

Make Him proud!

Singles Ministry

*Although the Proverbs 31 woman was married, your goal, if you desire to be married or remarried, should be to please God and to allow Him to prepare you. Therefore, I was led to include this chapter for the singles. The beginning sections will deal with a number of the pitfalls, issues and stumbling blocks you may encounter as you move through this season. **This section ends with a step-by-step guide of how to navigate the waters of being a single Christian and is totally appropriate for a singles ministry group.***

Get Out Of My Way

I distinctly remember an instant during my 'season of singleness,' when I just got downright mad; angry even! I was mad, because I kept making the same mistake over and over again. I would meet someone, fall in 'lust', maybe love, but not the kind God intended and end up having sex in some form or another, only to find out (not too long afterwards) that he was not the one either. This cycle continued over and over again. I wasted many, many years. I pray you won't.

Maybe you need proof or some background to go along with this story (that is all true, mind you) to help you get angry, too.

Donnell: I met Donnell one summer when I was newly divorced. The devil sent him packaged just right. A 'friend introduced him to me' so my assumption (wrongly) was that he must be a good man. We hung out all summer. D was here on military duty, and we grew close really fast. Well, I decided that things were going so great that I wanted to take the connection even deeper.

Please note: **I DECIDED.** God was nowhere in my thought processes.

I was a Christian at this point, but still had one foot in the world and was not totally sold out. I felt like God could handle all of my other stuff, issues, concerns, but since I had continually been let down by men, He was not able to fix this, so I would handle it myself. Not so much…

So the night came for me to facilitate our 'deeper connection' and things went off without a hitch.

Side Note: All day long, in the Spirit, I could hear this voice audibly saying, *"Humble yourself under the mighty hand of God!"*

What?! Oh well. I moved on with my plan. This was going to be great!

Donnell left to go back home with the promise of visits and even a potential move for me to be where he was. I began to search for places to work and live. Wow, could it be? My birthday was later that week, so I anxiously waited for him to call. Excitement mounted daily. My birthday came and went and there was no phone call. Two days later he called me. I was so excited, until I heard the sound of his voice. He told me that his wife made him call to tell me that he could no longer have a relationship with me. And as he spoke, I could hear their baby crying in the background. Needless to say, I was devastated. I told him to never call me again and hung up the phone.

After the tears were done, I began to revisit all of our conversations. He said he was not married and he did not have children. I had even prayed about this man; how did I miss this? All of the outward signs pointed to Donnell being "the one." Also, he had mentioned God and he was a friend of a friend.

The Problem: I prayed about him but I had no intention of waiting on God to answer. I was still focused on what I wanted and not what God wanted.

John: I was really walking strong with the Lord this time and was doing well abstaining from sex, although I was still struggling with masturbation.

Side Note: Anything other than holiness is an open door or "a little fox." **Song of Solomon 2:15 (NIV)** states: "*Catch all the foxes, those little foxes, before they ruin the vineyard of love, for the grapevines are blossoming!*"

A friend of mine called and asked me to attend a homecoming function with her. Initially, I didn't want to go. I was actually trying to live right, trying to live holy before God, and I was working in the church, and just feeling good about where I stood spiritually. Against my better judgment, I went to the party. From the time I got there, I was like a 'guy magnet' and not in a good way. I couldn't wait to get out of there. Just as I was about to leave, I met John. He asked me for my number and I gave it to him.

I don't know why I said yes, because he was not even my type, but that's how the devil gets us. He catches us off guard. But God has warned us in advance through His Word about the consequences of temptation and of sin and in our language (the one just between Him and us, individually). He had warned me in a vision almost a year before, but I didn't know what it meant and I walked on in ignorance.

"Let no one say when he is tempted, 'I am being tempted by God,' for God cannot be tempted with evil, and he himself tempts no one. But each person is tempted when he is lured and enticed by his own desire. Then desire when it has conceived gives birth to sin, and sin when it is fully grown brings forth death." **James 1:13-15 (ESV)**

I sexually fell again and this time, it came with a price. During this time, I was preparing to go on a trip to Germany for work as well as to aid my pastor. Can you imagine?! God, do we have no fear of You?!

Prior to leaving, and after the 'fall,' I began to have some "female issues," so I went to the doctor, who was also a friend of mine. I explained to the physician that I needed to have some tests done and a prescription because I was going overseas and didn't want to be without any necessary medication.

So we ran the tests and things came back fine, or so I thought. While in Germany, I realized that the Spirit of the Lord had departed from me and that the medical issue was probably not going to just go away. I didn't have any physical reason to believe this, only a gut feeling. The day after I returned home, my physician called to tell me that my tests had all come back negative, with the exception of one.

She said, "I'm sorry to tell you that you have been exposed to herpes."

I didn't know what to do. I was sick, disgusted, afraid, broken, all at the same time.

I called my pastor and my sister, and I later told my mother. I didn't tell anyone else. This was a Friday night, and we had church to attend. While I was there, a prophet came to me and said in my ear, "Is there anything too hard for the Lord?"

Then another prophet came and whispered in my ear, "God has healed you."

I didn't receive my healing, at first, because I felt as though I didn't deserve it. Over the next two months, I went for a second and third evaluation and had to take a round of antiviral drugs. It was *so* humiliating and embarrassing having to go to the pharmacy. I lost a relationship after I shared the diagnosis; I saw actual herpes sores on myself. There's no way that I was healed.

Between the second and third doctor's visit, I had a talk with God and explained to Him that I wanted to believe and receive my healing, but I was struggling with the guilt and condemnation.

He reminded me of His Word in **Romans 8:1 (NIV)**: *"Therefore, there is now no condemnation for those who are in Christ Jesus."*

I received this Word and my healing on the same day. On the third visit, my tests were all negative and to this day, I have never had to deal with this again. I can say like **Job** said in verse **42:5 (NIV)**, *"My ears had heard of you but now my eyes have seen you."*

Hallelujah!

There are so many things I want to say to you, and it is hard to get all my thoughts straight, but I will try:

1. You need to just get 'pure-t' mad with the devil and tell him you are not taking his mess anymore.

2. Next, you need to confess to yourself about your own shortcomings and faults, such as always needing a man, trying to fill your voids with men or things.

3. You need to confess to God and repent for not letting Him be your first love. In truth, He is your husband until you are married, but in the spirit realm, we as believers are His Bride. So, what you must realize is that each time you had sex with anyone, including yourself, you were committing adultery with God.

4. You need to get mad with anyone currently in your life, who is defiling you and keeping you from walking with God in the beauty of holiness and hindering you from fulfilling the assignment God has placed on your life.

5. Get up and **DON'T LOOK BACK! DON'T LOOK LEFT OR RIGHT!** *"A song of ascents. I lift up my eyes to the hills--where does my help come from?"* **Psalm 121:1 (NIV)**

Beloved, I could tell you multiple stories of multiple falls, but what I want you to know more than anything is God can and will - if you will. If you will humble yourself under His mighty hand, if you will seek His face and seek to do His will and wait for His answer, if you will get downright mad at anyone who tries to defile you, persuade you or hinder you in your walk with Christ, you WILL BE triumphant. God will change your life, He will heal your body, and He will turn your mourning into dancing!

Don't believe me? He says it in His Word:

- *"If my people, who are called by my name, will humble themselves and pray and seek my face and turn from their wicked ways, then will I hear from heaven and will forgive their sin and will heal their land,"* **2 Chronicles 7:14 (NIV)**.

- *"You have turned my mourning into joyful dancing. You have taken away my clothes of mourning and clothed me with joy,"* **Psalm 30:11 (NLT)**

- *"Humble yourselves, therefore, under God's mighty hand, that he may lift you up in due time."* **1Peter 5:6 (NIV)**

What are your thoughts?

_____

_____

_____

_____

Gurlz Just Wanna Have Fun!

I recently attended a meeting with a group from my church, and one of the attendees made a statement and asked a question at the same time: "A woman I was speaking to told me that our souls are with the Lord, and we are in the flesh. Therefore, it's not possible to not sin since we are in the flesh."

What?!

My desire is to always respond in the way God would have me to respond, no matter how much I want to address people in the flesh. Therefore, my response was, "You need to just be honest with yourself first. Do you really even desire to be holy, to live a sin free life? Or do you want to just have fun knowing that *every time* you willingly sin and then repent, God is going to forgive?"

Paul speaks on this in **Galatians 5:13 (MSG)**: *"It is absolutely clear that God has called you to a free life. Just make sure that you don't use this freedom as an excuse to do whatever you want to do and destroy your freedom. Rather, use your freedom to serve one another in love; that's how freedom grows."*

If we're honest, we have all lived a life that was not always pleasing to God. However, once we become saved, we must and should desire to turn away from those things, which cause us to sin and to walk in righteousness. It is a process and it's not always easy. However, it is doable - IF we have a made-up mind, and we walk according to the direction of the Holy Spirit and not in our flesh or our own understanding.

That woman from church felt as though sin is inevitable and therefore, it is impossible for us to be free from the bondage of sin. Rather, we should let ourselves off of the hook, because God will continually forgive us.

Well, the devil is a liar and a defeated foe!

Paul in **Galatians 5:10-25** talks about "walking in the Spirit." To paraphrase, this scripture states we should walk in the Spirit so that we don't fulfill the lust of the flesh; and that the Spirit and the flesh are at war with one another, so that we don't do the things WE want. And if we walk according to the Spirit we are no longer under the law.

Remember, the works of the flesh are evident and are: adultery, fornication, uncleanness, lewdness, idolatry, sorcery, hatred, contentions, jealousies, outbursts of wrath, selfish ambitions, dissensions, heresies, envy, murders, drunkenness revelers and the like. Those who practice such things will not see the kingdom of God.

In contrast, the fruit of the Spirit are love, joy, peace, longsuffering, kindness, goodness, faithfulness, gentleness, self-control, against such there is no law.

The most crucial aspect of proof is in **Galatians 5:24 (NLT)**, which states, *"Those who belong to Christ Jesus have nailed the passions and desires of their sinful nature to his cross and crucified them there."*

This says to me that WE have responsibility and the *ability* to NOT willfully sin. So what is the problem? Further, verse 25 concludes the matter by stating if we live in the Spirit let us also walk in the Spirit. Be transformed by the renewing of your mind. Do something different, stop doing the same thing and expecting a different result!

Finally, as God has said, Be Holy for I AM Holy...I AM is Holy.

The Dating Pool and Kissing Frogs (Don't drown in there!)

The inspiration for this chapter came from a discussion I had with a young friend of mine who is like a little sister to me. She was mentioning some of her dating issues and I was reminded about my own experiences. I was thinking about how glad I am that I am no longer in the "dating pool". I thought I would drown in there, and Lord knows I kissed *way too many* frogs, toads, tadpoles and icky, squishy, well...you get the picture.

Pause for the Cause: STOP where you are, exit to the right of the dating pool before you drown or kiss another frog who is NOT your husband!

My friend told me, "There is this guy, and I can't get him off my mind. We dated for awhile last year and things didn't work out because I found out he had a girlfriend."

When I asked if he was Christian or saved, she responded, "No, he's _____ (you can fill in the blank). But we were really good friends, and we understood one another in terms of the industry we worked in and the crazy hours we both kept. When we got together we both knew that we were not looking for a committed relationship, and we promised each other that we wouldn't develop feelings for one another."

WHAT?!

Okay, first of all, I know God meant for us to be friends because this scenario sounded all too familiar, just with different actors and actresses and LOTS OF DRAMA!

I want to keep my response short, sweet and to the point:

- **The husband is supposed to find a wife.** You don't have to look for him or wonder if it is he or try to make it him. You will know beyond a shadow of a doubt if this is the man that God has sent. Don't try and make it work - circles and squares do not go together and neither do believers and unbelievers. God has already given you the key to knowing at least one way to tell if this is your mate - they love, believe and belong to God, too.

- **Kissing frogs and friends with benefits.** If the man you are interested in, dating or what have you, is willing to be a 'friend with benefits' or allow you to be anything other than a wife, then I won't look at him sideways. I'll look at you sideways. A man of God (i.e. your husband) would NEVER disrespect you or defile you in such a manner, because a true man of God will recognize that not only are you worth waiting until marriage, he would not dare defile the holy temple of God, which you both are. Your bodies don't belong to you; they belong to God.

- **If he is willing to defile you, then he is NOT the one.** Additionally, if you have been engaged for longer than three to six months or your wedding date is some ridiculous future date or he wants to just live together and try things out, please refer back to "*Pause for the Cause*" and respond accordingly.

- **Lastly, why would you lie or try to convince yourself that you are okay with having a lackluster, half-baked relationship when you know that it is your desire to be married?**

Moreover, how do you think that you have any control over your emotions when you have no control over your body or even your thought life on most days?!

Put the frog down and get out of the pool! Wait on your husband to find you. If you decide to take your own way, prepare for warts (herpes, consequences and the like); potential drowning and a lifetime in a stale, stagnant, stinky pond.

You choose.

Masturbation

Well let's just get this out of the way. Yes, I did say the "M" word and yes, it is somewhat embarrassing. However, as Christians, this is something that we *rarely,* if ever, discuss and it's something that has to be put out there.

I have been a single Christian and I am around many single Christians. And this is the way many are "getting by" in the midst of waiting for their spouse to show up. I want to tell you right now S-T-O-P, in the name of Jesus! When you perform masturbation, you are defiling yourself, your temple - which God dwells in - and you are committing adultery against God.

I do not want to appear to be 'high and mighty' or, God forbid, a hypocrite; therefore, I want you to know that this was something God had to deliver me from. So I know that He can and will deliver you, if you give it over to Him.

As plain as I can say it, God created SEX, in any form, for the sanctity of marriage. However, many Christians have been lulled into believing that this is okay. I know that I may receive some pushback on this. However, I am going to take you to the Word and let you duke it out with Jesus! My main reference for this is, of course, the Bible.

Many Christians have trouble with the subject of God's views on masturbation because it is not 'specifically' discussed in the Bible. Drugs aren't mentioned either, but does this mean that we should all just have a free for all?!

1 Corinthians 6:18 (NIV) further confirms this, saying that unlawful sexual relations defile our own bodies: *"Flee from sexual immorality. All other sins a man commits are outside his body, but he who sins sexually sins against his own body."*

When I was single, I rationalized that it was okay to masturbate since I was not "having sex" with anyone and therefore, I was maintaining God's precepts. Further, I had a girlfriend who had been walking with the Lord for a long time and she was a big advocate of this. Because I was weak and didn't know the Word, I thought it must be okay. Not so.

This is why we have to know the Word of God for ourselves and apply it to our life regardless of what others do. The spirit of lust is like a drug and will lead you deeper and deeper into immorality and other areas satan would take you. This spirit is like a bottomless pit. It is NEVER satisfied.

If you struggle with masturbation and other areas of sexual immorality, consider going on a consecration fast. The Bible tells us: *"Jesus replied, "This kind can be cast out only by prayer."* **Mark 9:29 (NLT)**

Homosexuality

This chapter was definitely a challenge to write, because going in I had my own personal feelings regarding the issue of homosexuality and found that each time I tried to write, I had extreme writer's block.

Shortly after beginning this chapter, I was out with a couple of girlfriends both whom are Christians. During our discussion, I began to share my feelings of being 'stuck' on this chapter. The conversation that ensued helped me to see the root of the problem and why I was unable to move forward in writing or in relationships with those who profess to be homosexual.

When the Lord gave me this chapter it was somewhat shocking to my husband. He wondered what homosexuality had to do with helping women find their way home or get closer to becoming the Proverbs 31 woman. I explained to him that the purpose of this book was to find those along the journey who have lost their way to get back on the path God has revealed through His truth and to make it safely home; thus taking on their position as a woman after God's own heart. Given that, this topic definitely falls in line.

Further, when the Holy Spirit revealed this chapter to me, I clearly heard Him say that many times, women who have been hurt repeatedly by men end up, in some cases, seeking relationships with women because they are convinced that all men are bad and will never love them the way they want, need or deserve. This is a lie. Some women have been molested and therefore were caught up in sexual perversion against their will.

On a different note, a friend of mine, who dabbled in homosexuality stated, "There are women who have always wanted to be with women and have never been with a man." At the time of this writing, I don't have clarity or anything to write at present to address this other than to say, the Lord's approach to sin is all the same regardless of the circumstances.

What was interesting is that this same friend suggested that I spend some time speaking to women who have dabbled in homosexuality or who are living this lifestyle daily. She went on to say that she felt this would enlighten me somewhat as to how women in this lifestyle actually think and feel. Not all women turn to women out of hurt; some have never known anything other than a desire to be with women from a very young age, she said. I have asked the Lord that if that be His will, to send women He would have me speak to and potentially minister to with regard to homosexuality.

My true dilemma in much of this is how to love someone - a family member or friend - and not imply through this love that I accept this lifestyle. Well, what my friend said, which shouldn't have shocked me was, "You just love them!"

She was right. Isn't this what Jesus would do?

She went on to say, "Why do we love the liar, the backslider, the adulterer, the slanderer, etc. Yet find it almost impossible to accept someone caught in or struggling with the sin of homosexuality when one sin is NO greater than another sin. And, instead of trying to show them the truth in love, we damn them all to hell and walk away as though our job as a Christian has been accomplished."

Now, let me explain. I am not an advocate of any sin. I myself am a sinner, saved by grace, and have sinned and come short of the glory of God. I strive daily to be holy as God is holy and can only do so by God's grace. Hence, on my best days, I am still only as a filthy rag before God. As such, my god-ordained task is to share the truth of God's love with all men and women, not to make them accept it or live it…period.

1 Corinthians 3:6 (NLT) says: *"I planted the seeds in your hearts, and Apollos watered it, but it was God who made it grow."*

The truth we share may not blossom or be illuminated in their hearts until much later. So our job is not to change them, but to present God and His Word, so that He may be glorified. My friend shared a piece of wisdom with me that I felt was mind blowing. She said when we plant the seed, we must plant the right seed and it must be planted correctly. The right seed is love; the correct way is in truth. Therefore, my job - our job - as believers in Christ is to plant the seed and to share the truth in love. Anything other than that is control and judgment. Jesus constantly told the truth to His disciples, to the naysayer and to the sinners. But He always offered them love, eternal life and a chance to repent and be forgiven.

An important note is that Jesus *listened.*

Although, He didn't agree with sin, He always understood. It was and is ALWAYS up to the person on the receiving end if they will receive Him or not. Many of us have been guilty of cutting our brothers and sisters, making them feel guilty, manipulating them, or just rejecting them entirely. None of these equal the "loving kindness" expressed and exemplified by Jesus.

The way of Christ is unconditional love, understanding and truth.

I have been guilty of trying to make people repent and for that I repent and ask God to forgive me in Jesus' name. I don't have a Heaven or hell to place anyone in.

One of the aforementioned friends shared this during our time together and I feel as though it is exceptionally relevant. She said the way we should approach anyone is through TRUTH, LOVE AND UNDERSTANDING. We beat people over the head with the truth of God's Word, but we don't add any love to it. Therefore, it is of no effect.

1 Corinthians 13:1 (NLT) tells us: *"If I speak in the tongues of men and of angels, but have not love, I am only a resounding gong or a clanging cymbal."*

Jesus always gives or leaves us with hope. He always tells us, we don't have to stay this way; whereas people want to break each other into pieces and walk away saying, "I have done God's work."

Now, don't get me wrong, the Bible says the Word of God is *"living and active. Sharper than any double-edged sword, it penetrates even to dividing soul and spirit, joints and marrow; it judges the thoughts and attitudes of the heart."*[12] The purpose of the Word is to reveal the hard and heal with love.

What I want anyone reading this right now to know is homosexuality is not God's choice for you. He has the ability to forgive you, heal you and restore you, if you only ask. If you choose to continue on in this lifestyle choice, it will ultimately lead to judgment by God, as this is the consequence of *all* sin. I love you enough to tell you the truth. Below are some scriptures that may help you as you consider your path:

"But nothing unclean will ever enter it, nor anyone who does what is detestable or false, but only those who are written in the Lamb's book of life." **Revelations 21:27 (ESV)**

"Everyone whom the Father gives me will come to me. I will never turn away anyone who comes to me." **John 6:37 (GWT)**

"Flee from sexual immorality. All other sins a person commits are outside the body, but whoever sins sexually, sins against their own body. Do you not know that your bodies are temples of the Holy Spirit, who is in you, whom you have received from God? You are not your own; you were bought at a price. Therefore honor God with your bodies." **1 Corinthians 6:18-20 (NIV)**

"Jesus replied, "This kind can be cast out only by prayer." **Mark 9:29 (NLT)** Accept Jesus' unconditional love as a means of healing and deliverance.

"For God so loved the world that he gave his one and only Son, that whoever believes in him shall not perish but have eternal life," **John 3:16 (NIV)**

Read **Joshua 24:15 (MSG):** *"If you decide that it's a bad thing to worship GOD, then choose a god you'd rather serve—and do it today. Choose one of the gods your ancestors worshiped from the country beyond the river, or one of the gods of the Amorites, on whose land you're now living. As for me and my family, we'll worship GOD."*

---

[12] Hebrews 4:12 (NIV)

Sex without marriage is a sin... period. And God is clarifying that when this act does take place, it is to be between a man and his wife in the sanctity of marriage.

Beloved, it is up to you now. The choice is yours.

Premarital Sex

This section can be used as a part of a singles conference workshop. It was co-authored with my husband Dalton J. Carter. We met while we were leading the Singles Ministries at our respective churches.

We live in a time and in a society that is all about freedom- freedom of expression, freedom of speech, freedom to life, liberty and the pursuit of happiness. However, as children of God, this particular brand of freedom doesn't apply to us.

In other chapters, we have discussed or will discuss holiness and purity. However, I felt as though the Lord was leading me to include a section on premarital sex. Understandably, many single Christians struggle with this and have questions regarding God's thoughts about premarital sex, such as what is allowed and what is not.

As a single Christian, I met many women and men who were Christians and were of the mindset that they could have sex and that it was acceptable to God because, they had an understanding with Him and He knew their heart. To that I say, "The devil is a liar!"

God is not a man and is therefore not required to enter into some sort of agreement with us. His Word stands true and is specific as to what His thoughts are regarding sex before marriage and it is our job to obey to the best of our abilities. On the subject of Him knowing our heart, this is what the Bible says in **Jeremiah 17:9-10 (MSG)**

"The heart is hopelessly dark and deceitful, a puzzle that no one can figure out. But I, God, search the heart and examine the mind. I get to the heart of the human. I get to the root of things. I treat them as they really are, not as they pretend to be."

Two words came to me as I was writing: Discipline and Commitment.

In **1 Corinthians 9:27 (NLT)**, the Apostle Paul tells us that he disciplines his body and therefore we can and must also: *"I discipline my body like an athlete, training it to do what it should. Otherwise, I fear that after preaching to others I myself might be disqualified."*[13]

Adding to this, the apostle Peter, in **2 Peter 1:10**, tells us to make our calling and election sure. What he is saying is if we neglect to enhance ourselves and grow in the virtues of virtue,

---

[13] Reference scriptures: Romans 6:18, Romans 8:13 and Jeremiah 6:30.

knowledge, self-control, perseverance and godliness, we may fall back into sin and be worse off than before. To do this, he tells us to examine ourselves and to ask ourselves if our living exemplifies Christ whom we claim to believe in and live as. This is done by disciplining our body as we have discussed previously.

How can you discipline your body?

_____

_____

How can you remain committed to living a godly life and therefore abstaining from premarital sex?

_____

_____

_____

The next section will focus on a step-by-step guide of how single Christians can navigate the sometimes testy waters of singlehood.

Embrace Your Singleness

I was standing in the kitchen one morning and I heard the Lord saying, *"Embrace your singleness."*

What?!

He continued, *"You are missing out on life, on fun, and opportunities by lamenting about being single. Go out and live, but continue to seek me and maintain holiness."*

I mean, can you relate? I can. The majority of my 'single season' conversations centered on my being single and this just discolored my life in so many ways. I am certain this was not pleasing or glorifying to God. I beg you, please stop right now! Just think about it, you have friends all over the place (I mean the saved, sensible friends, of course. If this is untrue, then this is a good time to make new friends). You could be traveling, spa-timing, and just taking time to truly learn and love you. Take this time to just be and to grow closer to God. Do you have hobbies or a list of things you would like to do before you die? Go exploring, different places, foods, places, etc.

Admittedly, the season of singleness was one of the most difficult as well as rewarding seasons of my life to navigate. As a single Christian, you have the responsibility to manage yourself according to godly standards. For many Christians, this can be a slippery slope.

Note: I refer to it as a "season," because, unless God has called you to singleness, then you will eventually be married and therefore, singleness is only going to last for a season.

Early on, we discussed the importance of accepting Jesus as your personal Lord and Savior. Part of this acceptance involves putting Him first. Let's apply the *principle of first fruits* here.

Essentially, *first fruits* involve giving God the first and best of whatever you have. As a single Christian, your first fruits are your body, your focus, your time, and so on. Remember that in this season (and every other season in the life of a Christian), God is our husband.

"For your Maker is your husband--the LORD Almighty is his name--the Holy One of Israel is your Redeemer; he is called the God of all the earth.." **Isaiah 54:5 (NIV)**

Accept Christ

Prayer of Salvation *(Pray this out loud):* "*God in Heaven, I come to you in the name of Jesus. I confess I have not lived my life for you. But I am glad to know I can change that. I have decided to accept that Jesus is your son, and that He died on the cross and rose again from the dead, so I might have eternal life and the blessings of life now. Jesus come into my heart, be my Savior, be my Lord. From this day forward, and to the best of my ability, I will live my life for you. In Jesus' name, I pray. Amen.*"

Next, you must commit yourself and your life to God by asking Him to clean you up. This process requires a great deal of work on your part. We will journey through this process in stages, but first you must repent.

"I correct and discipline everyone I love. Take this seriously, and change the way you think and act." Revelation 3:19 (GWT)

Allow the Holy Spirit to reveal the sin in your life to you and ask God for forgiveness and pray, according to **Psalm 51**.

God, Clean Me Up

Walk in the beauty of holiness. **1 Peter 1:13-16 (NIV)** reminds us, *"Therefore, prepare your minds for action; be self-controlled; set your hope fully on the grace to be given you when Jesus Christ is revealed. As obedient children, do not conform to the evil desires you had when you lived in ignorance. But just as he who called you is holy, so be holy in all you do; for it is written: 'Be holy, because I am holy.'"*

And **2 Corinthians 7:1 (NIV)** states, *"Since we have these promises, dear friends, let us purify ourselves from everything that contaminates body and spirit, perfecting holiness out of reverence for God."*

- **Separate yourself from the world.** In order for you to continue to be cleansed, you must make a firm and resolute decision to change the company that you keep; unless you are the one that other people need to separate from. **1 Corinthians 5:6** tells us, *"a little leavens the whole thing."(paraphrased)* And **2 Corinthians 6:17** exhorts us to *"Therefore come out from among them and be separate, says the Lord. Touch no unclean thing, and I will receive you."*

Areas you may be struggling in include going to the club - dancing; bike clubs, social clubs, friends with benefits, hanging around people who don't share your same beliefs, or getting rid of people in your life who are stumbling blocks.

- **Have an accountability partner.** God has not intended us to be alone on this journey or in life. He has sent fellow Christians to help us and intends for us to help them, as well. **Galatians 6:1-2(NIV)** tells us, *"Brothers, if someone is caught in a sin, you who are spiritual should restore him gently. But watch yourself, or you also may be tempted. Carry each other's burdens, and in this way you will fulfill the law of Christ."* **James 5:16 (NIV)** tells us, *"Therefore confess your sins to each other and pray for each other so that you may be healed. The prayer of a righteous man is powerful and effective."*

When I was dating, my accountability partner was my sister. I let her know when I had a date, who it was, where I was going and when I was coming back. This may seem like a lot to deal with; however, I wanted to maintain my integrity at ALL costs.

- **Use the Holy Spirit as your wingman.** The Bible establishes that the Lord has sent the Holy Spirit as a helper and comforter.[14] Ask the Holy Spirit to guide all of your actions. *"No test or temptation that comes your way is beyond the course of what others have had to face. All you need to remember is that God will never let you down; he'll never let you be pushed past your limit; he'll always be there to help you come through it."* **1 Corinthians 10:13 (MSG)**

And **Proverbs 3:5-6 (KJV)** states, *"Lean not to thine own understanding, but in all thy ways acknowledge him and he shall direct thy paths."*

---

[14] 1 Corinthians 10:13; 10:26; John 14:16 and John 15:26

- **Put on your armor.** Part of your SUPERb woman supply list includes the armor of God. Previously, we discussed the importance of arming ourselves for war. You must clothe yourself daily in order to maintain cleanliness and holiness- you will need it to withstand.[15]

- **Put away fleshly desires.** Commit to discontinue masturbation, watching pornography and any other activity that feeds your flesh.

Get Your Mind Right- It's NOT All About You

As a single Christian it is very easy to fall into a pattern of self-centeredness and self-preoccupation. However, as a child of God, you must remember it is not all about you. I realize this might require a huge mind shift on your part, but you must continue to grow in the ways of God.

He tells us in **Romans 12:2 (NIV)** to be transformed by the renewing of our minds and to make decisions based solely according to His will not on emotions. You must remember that you are not only getting *yourself* together for you, you are being prepared for ministry.[16] Ministry is multifaceted. It involves ministry in the Kingdom of God, ministry in marriage - if that is your desire - and preparation to meet God when He comes back.

Use Your Sword Daily

When Jesus was led by the Holy Spirit into the wilderness to be tempted by the devil, He used His sword at each attack.[17] There is power in the Word of God and it is the only thing the devil recognizes. Additionally, when God hears His Word being spoken, He sends power to galvanize change on our behalf.

Using the Word of God effectively involves praying God's Word[18] asking God for wisdom, [19]and then taking this Word and applying it to your life on a daily basis.

*For assistance with learning to pray the Word of God go to the **Daily Prayer Journal**, located at the end of the book.

Isaiah 55:11(KJV) confirms that God's Word is powerful and that He backs it up: *"So shall my word be that goeth forth out of my mouth: it shall not return unto me void, but it shall accomplish that which I please, and it shall prosper in the thing whereto I sent it."*

---

[15] Ephesians 6:11
[16] Matthew 25:1-13, Hebrews 5:12
[17] Matthew 4:1
[18] Isaiah 55:11
[19] James 1:5

Ask God daily to give you wisdom, knowledge and understanding to study His Word and apply it to your life.

James 1:5 (KJV) tells us, *"If any of you lack wisdom, let him ask of God, that giveth to all men liberally, and upbraideth not; and it shall be given him."*

Hide God's Word in your heart that you might not sin against Him[20].

Get Busy

This season is critical in your walk with Christ because your whole focus can and should be devoted to pleasing God and finding out His will and purpose for your life. The Apostle Paul] tells us in **1 Corinthians 7:34 (NIV)** , *"An unmarried woman or virgin is concerned about the Lord's affairs: Her aim is to be devoted to the Lord in both body and spirit."(partial use of scripture)*

What is it that God has called you to do?

_____

_____

_____

One area of ministry that is directly in line with God's will for all of His children is for us to spread the Word of God and lead others to Christ.

Evangelism: The winning or revival of personal commitments to Christ; militant or crusading zeal.

The definition of evangelism, given by the Archbishop of Canterbury for the Anglican Church, is: "To so present Christ in the power of the Holy Spirit that men shall come to put their trust in God, Through Him and, accepting Him as their Lord, seek to serve Him in the fellowship of His Church."

What can you do to "get busy"?

_____

_____

Begin to evangelize to those around you - friends, family and co-workers.

"Andrew, Simon Peter's brother, was one of the two who heard what John had said and who had followed Jesus. 41The first thing Andrew did was to find his brother Simon and tell him, "We have found the Messiah" (that is, the Christ). 42And he brought him to Jesus. **"John 1:40-42 (NIV)**

---

[20] Psalm 119:11

This may not be an easy feat, but allow me to address some obvious questions:

This sounds easy but how do I reach those that are close to me? They know all my dirt and the life I "used" to live.

Use your experiences, gifts, testimonies to bring others to Christ. This is your personal testimony, the why and how you know that Jesus is real in your life.

1 Peter 3:15-17 (NIV) *"But in your hearts set apart Christ as Lord. Always be prepared to give an answer to everyone who asks you to give the reason for the hope that you have. But do this with gentleness and respect,* **16**keeping a clear conscience, so that those who speak maliciously against your good behavior in Christ may be ashamed of their slander. **17**It is better, if it is God's will, to suffer for doing good than for doing evil.*"*

What if they don't receive me or talk about me for bringing the Gospel?

My favorite saying is, "Keep it moving!!!"

"And if a town refuses to welcome you, shake its dust from your feet as you leave to show that you have abandoned those people to their fate." **Luke 9:5 (NLT)**

A huge part of being single, involves combating loneliness. You can avoid this by getting busy for God. Attend church events and mingle with other church singles groups. *"Let us not give up meeting together, as some are in the habit of doing, but let us encourage one another- and all the more as you see the Day approaching.* **"Hebrews 10:19-25 (NIV)**

It's easy to get off track with being a single parent, business owner, and full time student. Being offended or even disenchanted with the church can also keep you from fellowshipping with His people. Don't let that be a stumbling block for you.

"Abide in Me, and I in you, As the branch cannot bear fruit of itself, unless it abides in the vine, neither can you, unless you abide in Me." **John 15:4 (ESV)**

Get involved in small group studies, meet one-on-one with the Pastor or staff and express your true feelings. Talk about personal experiences with being offended in church, or just being ready to throw in the towel. These are great exercises to do until God speaks to you about where He wants you and what He wants you to do.

Stay busy working for the kingdom of God as well as pursuing personal goals

Idle:

1. Denotes inactive, unfruitful, barren; or

2. Lacking worth or basis

"Besides, they get into the habit of being idle and going about from house to house. And not only do they become idlers, but also gossips and busybodies, saying things they ought not to." **1 Timothy 5:11-15 (NIV)**

Do you know anyone like this? Is this you? This passage of scripture speaks about young widows in particular but notice verse 11. It talks about their sensual desires overcoming their dedication to Christ. I believe this Word could also be applied to much more than young widows.

Final Note: Understand that this is a process! Work for God right now. Don't wait for Him to make you perfect. He will perfect you as you work for Him.

Children

BITTERNESS
ADULTERY
REBELLION
GREED
INDECISION
CONDEMNATION
LUST

"Her children stand and bless her. Her husband praises her."
Proverbs 31:28 (NLT)

Don't Hate...Congratulate!

What can I say…first of all when I started this book, four years ago, I wasn't married and I didn't have children. In 2009, the Lord blessed me with a husband and a 10-year-old son on the same day.

What in the world?!

The Lord had given me a Word through His Prophet that I was going to have a husband and a son. However, I thought He meant that I would give birth to a son. Well, turns out I was going to have child, although he was older, because God had placed me in his life to help him to become who God had intended him to be and to help birth the seed that God had placed in him.

Early on, my husband said to me, "You think that you have something to teach Miles (our son), but there are things he may teach you."

I remember thinking, "Yeah right!"

I had a bit of an attitude problem. What did I say that for?! My son, who is now 12 years old, has taught me a number of things:

- How to love someone that I didn't give birth to.
- How to understand someone who I didn't give birth to, but am responsible for as a mom.
- How to keep my hands to myself when I want to choke the living daylights out of him!
- How much, as a mother, you will protect your child against enemies foreign and domestic.
- How it's just really NOT that serious.
- Learn how to build bridges to his birth mom so that our family can be unified and he can be whole.
- How to accept a whole other extended family, even if they don't accept you - at first.
- How to see him and accept him as Christ did for me.
- Children know A LOT more than we give them credit for.

There are more lessons, I'm sure, but the list would take over the book.

So here we are with our chapter on children. One word came immediately to mind when I came to this chapter—**Agape.** This is the area that my son and the Lord have worn me out with!

Agape: Unconditional love.

This applies to birth mothers, stepmothers, adopted mothers, grandmothers…you name it. This applies to you, you and you!

Let's take a look at what agape looks like. First off, **John 15:12-13 (NLT)** tells us, *"This is my commandment: Love each other in the same way I have loved you. There is no greater love than to lay down one's life for one's friends."*

This means that others, especially our family and children must become more important to us than we are to ourselves. Allow me to explain. God is not implying that we should not, as parents, take care of ourselves, He is saying that our main focus should not always be centered on our wants and needs, but the needs of others. And as we meet the needs of our families and brothers and sisters in Christ, God will supply all of our needs and wants.

Secondly, agape love does not extend from emotions or feelings, as many might presume. Agape love is based on a decision to love. God chose to love us, in spite of our mess and our lack of unworthiness to be loved.

John 15:16 (NIV) proves it: *"You did not choose me, but I chose you and appointed you to go and bear fruit--fruit that will last. Then the Father will give you whatever you ask in my name."*

Agape love gives because it wants to and does not demand love or anything else in return. I know, this is a TALL order but we can do it. We must do it. God gave us His example in Jesus dying on the cross for us. I have heard people say, "I'm not Jesus and that is just too much to ask."

I assure you, it isn't always easy, and whether our children were given to us by birth or marriage, God's grace is sufficient to keep us in all things. In the preceding chapters we discussed, marriage, singles and now children. The overarching theme is FAMILY and it all equals ministry. God ministers to us and we minister His love and ways to our children.

The key here is God ministers to us first. If you are not spending time with God, then you may not be ministering to your children in the way God intended, if at all. Think about this. Your relationship with your children reflects your relationship with God.

What should our relationship to Him look like: Parent to child. He is the parent and we are His children. He gave birth to us, nurtures and protects us, feeds us, clothes us, directs us, disciplines us, all with unconditional love. This is the example He has given us for our children. Are we living it?

Saving the topic of children for the last part of our discussion is weird, I know. As I was writing this book, I had the title, "Children" written down. However, I was unable to complete this section. I knew it was because of something I had not yet lived, learned or accepted. Thank God I passed the test (or at least got to the point of being able to write this).

While learning the ropes of my role as a step-mom, the Holy Spirit told me, *"Don't hate, congratulate!"* I know this does not sound grammatically correct nor is it intended to. The Holy Spirit does not operate by the rules of man. He is the embodiment of God and yes, God has a major sense of humor!

In any case, what the Spirit revealed to me was that I was hating on my son when I should have been congratulating him. I know this is shocking, but I am only human and I am a work in progress. My prayer up to the point of writing this has been, "Lord, help me to see my child as you see Him and help me to love Him as you love Him."

Now, praying this means that I am also going to have to live this and be tested in it. Lord help! Well, thank God for help. Daily, God has shown me how to love my child and how to look beyond what I see with my natural eyes or think with my natural mind so that I can love him in the ways he needs. If I keep trying to love him the way I think I should, or the way I think he needs, he will not get what God intended and I will be in disobedience.

Loving him looks like telling him that daily, even when he has done something I don't like (i.e. lying, ignoring me, disobeying what I have expressly told him to do). Loving him means speaking to him with dignity and respect. Loving him means celebrating his accomplishments and not magnifying his faults and failures; and loving him means disciplining and **disciplining** him as God does us. Whew! Pray for me as I am determined to get this right and I am determined that you will too. I will be praying.

Another thing the Holy Spirit spoke to me during this chapter was to ask Miles what he and other children would want parents to know. I was *shocked* by his response. He offered three original thoughts on what he thinks parents should know:

1. Children should respect their parents and parents should respect their children.

2. Children should obey their parents.

3. Parents should and need to be responsible for their children.

After hearing this, I fell in love with him! My desire is to celebrate him more than anything and to continue to love him in every way possible.

I will not hate, but will congratulate him every day as God does for me. What will you do?

For stepparents who may be reading this or even natural parents, who are believing God for additional children; my husband and I believe God for our own children. God has promised us this. At the time of writing this book, I am not pregnant. But I know that it is only a matter of time before I am. God has shown me our unborn children; they are living in the spiritual realm with Him and will soon manifest in the natural. They are with God and He is filling them with all they will need to survive their journey here on earth, so they can lead others home to Him. This is the key: God revealed to me last year that until I love the child He had given to me, I would not have the child(ren) He promised me. I must be faithful to my initial blessing in Miles and then our other blessings will come. God knows, I am working towards this end.

Much Agape love to you and your children and your children's children.

You Are Not Alone

Jesus never sent the disciples out alone. They were always together or in groups of two or more. Furthermore, He provided them with leadership and guidance in the form of Jesus Christ. Thus, God has not sent you out alone either. He has placed friends, leaders and His Word in your possession. Each of these persons has been designed, by God, to help you navigate this life - this journey - so that you reach home safely. Jesus, you have Him now; friends; leaders and the Bible (your ultimate road map).

Let's look at your friends first.

Jesus is the ULTIMATE friend

"I've told you these things for a purpose: that my joy might be your joy, and your joy wholly mature. This is my command: Love one another the way I loved you. This is the very best way to love. Put your life on the line for your friends. You are my friends when you do the things I command you. I'm no longer calling you servants because servants don't understand what their master is thinking and planning. No, I've named you friends because I've let you in on everything I've heard from the Father." **John 15:14 (MSG)**

Sistahfriends

Let's face it; you can't make it in this life alone. Sistahfriends are a mission essential! Sistahfriends come in many forms - mothers, aunties, sisters, cousins, or friends - who are like sisters. While Proverbs 31 doesn't specifically mention them, there must have been a moment when she sat down for a cup of coffee with her Sistahfriends and dished about her maid servants, her husband sitting around in the city gates or her children acting up. I don't care how blessed they called her, and I know she had to say at least once, "I do *everything* around here!"

God did not leave us here on Earth alone. He intended for us to have friends, Sistahfriends, like Mary and Martha; friends like Jesus and Lazarus; friends Jesus and John.

Many know the story of Naomi and Ruth, wherein, Naomi was left with her two daughter-in-laws after the death of her sons. Ruth, one of the daughter-in-laws, refused to leave her mother-in-law, entreating her, "Don't force me to leave you; don't make me go home. Where you go, I go; and where you live, I'll live. Your people are my people, your God is my God; where you die, I'll die, and that's where I'll be buried, so help me God—not even death itself is going to come between us!"[21]

---
[21] Ruth 1:16

Many women, especially those who have been consistently hurt and dumped on by 'so-called' friends, find it *very* difficult to manage female friendships. I insist this is something that you have *seriously* got to work on. *It is a must.* This concept of 'friendship' is so important that King Solomon mentions it in, **Proverbs 18:24 (NKJV)** which states, *"A man that hath friends must show himself friendly, and there is a friend that sticketh closer than a brother"*

There are two reasons why you need friends on your journey:

Friends can lead you to your destiny.

Ruth wanted to stay with Naomi, her mother and her friend, no matter what. As the story goes, Naomi led Ruth to Boaz, her husband. Are you a friend who would stick around until the end, through death, uncertainty, poverty or even through your friend finding the 'perfect' mate while you remained unmarried?

Friends can lead to untold blessings.

In **2 Kings 2:2, 4, 6**, we see where the Prophet Elijah's assistant Elisha refused to leave his side. Why is this? Commentators pointed out that many times throughout the Bible, a person on the brink of death would leave a blessing to the one staying behind (servants, children, etc.). Elisha was not about to let Elijah leave until he received his blessings.

Would you stay through adversity? Would you travel all over the world with your friend, no matter the costs? Are you willing to stick the friendship out to receive the blessing in the end, no matter the blessing, no matter the situation?

Friendly Checkup

Can you grasp this concept? It is a tragedy that there are billions of people on earth, and there are so many women, men and children who do not have one person they can call friend.

I do wonder whose fault this is.

Are you behaving in a friendly manner? Do people want to be in your space or do they run or cringe when they see you coming? Are you one of those people who are purposefully mean in spite of yourself? Do you have to control everybody? Are you selfish? Are you a friend?

What's your response?

_____

_____

_____

_____

Based on your conclusions, take a mental inventory of the "friends" God has placed in your life up to this point and determine if there are any friendships or relationships that need work.

Leaders

Remember the game "Follow the Leader," some of us used to play when we were little called? The game is played when a leader is assigned. The leader tells the group to start doing something (i.e. run, walk, dance, etc.) in any order he wants. Then the leader instructs the rest of the players to follow in doing whatever the leader does in the exact same way. Anyone who fails to do what the leader does is put out of the game.

The concept of leadership for us, as Christians, is the same. God is the head of our life, husbands are the head of wives and Pastors are the head of the church with all roads leading back to God. We simply must have a leader and be in submission by following. There are times in our life where we will be in the role of the leader. However, more often than not, someone is leading us.

The point here is this, leaders are an essential element in our journey and our lesson, among others is obedience, submission and love. God said, "If you love Me, you will obey Me." Regarding submission, **Romans 13:1-2 (NIV)** tells us, *"Let everyone be subject to the governing authorities, for there is no authority except that which God has established. The authorities that exist have been established by God. Consequently, whoever rebels against the authority is rebelling against what God has instituted, and those who do so will bring judgment on themselves."*

And finally, the love of God should compel us to do what is right and pleasing in His sight.

Where do you stand with the leaders in your life?

_____

_____

_____

Submission is more difficult the older you get because we tend to be less trusting and more questioning than when we were when we were younger. Children simply comply without question. God tells us, *"I tell you the truth, unless you change and become like little children, you will not enter the Kingdom of Heaven."*[22]

The Bible

The book of Genesis tells us that Jesus was the Word of God: *"In the beginning the Word already existed. The Word was with God, and the Word was God."*

When Jesus walked the earth, the Word of God was present upon the earth and lived among the people of that time. We now have Jesus as our Lord and Savior and the Word of God with us in the form of the Bible. Therefore, we are not alone on this journey, as we have a risen Lord and Savior as well as the Word of God to show us the way.

"Your Word is a lamp to my feet and light for my path. **"Psalm 119:105 (NIV)**

---

[22] Matthew 18:3

Shine Gurl! Shine!

Many of us never make it to our fullest potential because 'we hide our light under a bushel' so that others will not be uncomfortable.

Meditate on this poem by Marianne Williamson:

"Our deepest fear is not that we are inadequate. Our deepest fear is that we are powerful beyond measure. It is our light, not our darkness that most frightens us. We ask ourselves, who am I to be brilliant, gorgeous, talented, fabulous? Actually, who are you not *to be? You are a child of God. Your playing small does not serve the world. There is nothing enlightened about shrinking so that other people won't feel insecure around you. We are all meant to shine, as children do. We were born to make manifest the glory of God that is within us. It's not just in some of us; it's in everyone. And as we let our own light shine, we unconsciously give other people permission to do the same. As we are liberated from our own fear, our presence automatically liberates others." (Williamson, 1992)*

Shrinking Violets

The catalyst for this particular entry is a girlfriend of mine who recently shared with me that she has a habit that I believe many women and men have, and one that I used to suffer from. My goal is to help set you and other captives free from the syndrome of the "shrinking violet."

I found that this term most often referred to someone being shy. But I wanted to speak to the person who may or may not be shy, but who always holds back and hides their light under a bushel so that others' demons and jealous spirits will not become agitated. Essentially, this person is trying to please people and not allow God to be glorified. Well, the devil is a liar and defeated foe!

Shrink: To cower, to huddle, or to refrain as in to hold one's self back.

What this says to me is the person who is a shrinking violet is suffering from a number of things, with the main spirit being FEAR - False Evidence Appearing Real. I approached this by looking at the characteristics of a violet, which is characterized by *showy* petals in pink, white or purple. I ask you, do the words "shrinking" and "showy" even belong in the same sentence?!

Williamson said, "We ask ourselves, who am I to be brilliant, gorgeous, talented, fabulous? Actually, who are you *not* to be? You are a child of God. Your playing small does not serve the world."

There is nothing enlightened about shrinking so that other people won't feel insecure around you. Many times, we as women and men feel as though we should be or feel apologetic when something wonderful happens to us or we find ourselves in the midst of those who may not have the same level of education, socio-economic status; or even worse, we dumb ourselves down and minimize our accomplishments, so that others will not feel bad.

Well, I know that I have *a lot* to say about this; however, this is God's book so I will decrease so that He might increase. What does He say? What would Jesus do? He would tell you, *"Man shall not live by bread alone, but by every Word that proceedeth out of the mouth of God"* according to **Matthew 4:4 (partial use of scripture) (KJV)**

Moreover, the Word of God says, *"Ye are the light of the world. A city that is set on an hill cannot be hid"*[23]; and lastly, *"Let your light so shine before men, that they may see your good works, and glorify your Father which is in heaven."*[24]

Now let them talk about that!

In what area of your life do you need to 'let your light shine'?

_____

_____

_____

_____

Don't Sell Your Soul. Get Your Stuff Back! Choose Ye This Day!

There is an old saying that talks about selling your soul to the devil. What does this mean exactly? How does it apply to you? Well, this is the era of modern thinking and the devil isn't running around in an obvious manner (i.e. red, with a pitchfork and this snide look on his face). He has taken many forms: cell phones, laptops, passion parties, masturbation, excessive shopping, excessive debt, needing a man/woman or both to keep you warm, chasing dollars, you get the picture. We've all been or still are guilty. As I sat down to write this book, I think about how God has cleaned house in my life. He set me free from the bondage of an $80,000 job where I was literally sick and the gentiles just ran rampant.

In May 2009, I clearly heard the Lord say, *"Cut yourself loose."* He was referring to my job. FINALLY! Hallelujah! I had been praying, begging, believing and quitting mentally for Him to do this. Well, what happened next was just a shock! I thought God was releasing me so that I could pursue the goals I thought He'd given me, such as growing my consulting business and being rich and fabulous, as a result. Well, He had other plans.[25]

---

[23] Matthew 5:14
[24] Matthew 5:16
[25] Jeremiah 29:11

The first Monday of my newfound freedom, the Lord gave my husband a Word for me: *"Build my house."*

Hmmm…interesting. Okay, Lord, what does this mean? I was lead to **Haggai 1-2**.

Essentially, Haggai 1 and 2 deals with the call of God to His people to rebuild His temple. The people had become comfortable and complacent in the natural and had neglected the spiritual house of God, to the point that it was in ruins and God was not pleased.

As a result of God's stirring the spirit of Zerubbabel to rebuild the temple, every one came together and as a result, God declared that this house would be even greater than the former and He would return and restore those who had been led into captivity.

What?! So, I felt as though I understood. I should build my physical body, spiritual house, family, home, and ministry. That's a tall order, but God was not pleased. He said, *"Is it a time for me to live in a paneled house while His house lay in ruins?"* In the end, His glory would rest on the rebuilt house as well as His peace.

Time to go to work!

I did pretty well, or so I thought. The devil dangled two consulting gigs in front of me, which I took (including payment). Cool! But wait, God deals with me in dreams and visions and more and more I began to see that He was none to pleased with me.

"Lord, what did I do," I asked. I ate the apple, by deciding to serve money. I'd stopped building and I came down off of the wall and left my work undone. It took awhile and a lot of WASTED time, but I think I am back on task. I'm typing anyway…

In the between time of stepping down off my wall, I had to give the money back and cancel both contracts - *awkward!* God showed me myself and it was NOT cute. I wandered around for a LONG time; then I ended up in this cramped cocoon, where I only have my laptop. But at least I'm allowed to have visitors.

I did promise to do His will and I promised to bring YOU back right? My apologies, as it's *totally* not about me nor has it ever been. I said all of this to say, we sometimes sell our soul and follow after the apples the enemy dangles in our face, because they look good and they 'look' like God. And often we sow to our flesh, desires and plans, even though we know that God has called us and gifted us for something different, greater, and higher for Him.

I would like for you to do something for you. Take a moment to write down three to five things, people, and/or places you have sold your soul to:

1.
2.
3.
4.
5.

Now, if you are sincere, repent (Psalm 51) and ask the Holy Spirit to help you get back on track.

What are you supposed to be doing for Him?

_____

_____

_____

Why aren't you doing it?

_____

_____

_____

You may be thinking, "What about me? What about what I want?"

"But seek ye first the kingdom of God, and His righteousness; and ALL these things shall be added unto you." **Matthew 6:33 (KJV)**

Look this verse up and the references to see what it's actually saying. Write what you discover below.

_____

_____

_____

_____

Put On Your Big Kid Drawers!

I can definitely say that I was a person who was easily offended. My offense typically affected me in the form of hurt feelings and taking almost everything personally and internalizing *everything*. I was constantly sad or depressed. What a roller coaster!

The opposite end of that spectrum is the person who is easily offended and exhibits anger. This person is always mad or reacts by separating himself from those he or she feels has offended them. This is a spirit of control and is used by people as a means of making the offender pay for what they have done.

As you can see, the spirit of offense has a sister and her name is Control.

The crazy part here – and I mean that loosely - is when you're the victim of these spirits is that you fail to ever look at yourself to see if you have been guilty of offending others. It feels good to let yourself off the hook by assuming that you treat everyone with loving-kindness, and thus have never been the offender. However, if you are truly honest with yourself, you are just as guilty.

The Word of God proves this in **James 3:2 (KJV):** *"For in many things we offend all. If any man offend not in word, the same is a perfect man, and able also to bridle the whole body."*

Now, don't get me wrong, you may be the one who has come to the ability to bridle his whole body. If you haven't, then you are still capable of offending.

Characteristics of people who are easily offended are: Overly-sensitive, often defensive, argumentative, angry, always justifying their behaviors and reactions, people have to walk on eggshells around you, you are ruled by your emotions and you want to take everyone on the emotional roller coaster with you, you *always* have to have your way or there will be hell to pay; you *are always* in conflict with someone or something.

If any of these are you, I have some questions for you. What is your deal? Why are you ALWAYS in a bad mood? And I have two words for you: Grow Up!

1 Corinthians 13:11-12 (NLT) says, *"When I was a child, I spoke and thought and reasoned as a child. But when I grew up, I put away childish things. Now we see things imperfectly as in a cloudy mirror, but then we will see everything with perfect clarity. All that I know now is partial and incomplete, but then I will know everything completely, just as God now knows me completely."*

We must see everything through the eyes of love - agape love; the love of God and not the love we feel in the flesh.

"And I know that nothing good lives in me, that is, in my sinful nature. I want to do what is right, but I can't. **Romans 7:18 (NLT)**

In **1 Peter 2:1-3** (MSG) it states, *"So clean house! Make a clean sweep of malice and pretense, envy and hurtful talk. You've had a taste of God. Now, like infants at the breast, drink deep of God's pure kindness. Then you'll grow up mature and whole in God."*

Even babies eventually go from milk to meat. It is the same with us as Christians. As we mature in the Lord, we have to give up childish thoughts and behaviors.

Make a decision today that you will not be like those, who when they heard the Word responded with great enthusiasm. But there is such shallow soil of character that when the emotions wear off and some difficulty arrives, there is nothing to show for it.[26]

Decide today that you will examine yourself to determine the reason for offense. Has the person truly offended you? Or are you someone who has a 'victim' mentality and is offended at the slightest thing? Either way, strive to be at peace with all men, including yourself.

The flipside of the coin: Don't get on the ride!

You may not be the person with an attitude; you may be the one who is *always* getting on someone else's emotional rollercoaster. If this is you, **please don't get on the ride!**

This phrase was born out of a conversation I had on more than one occasion with several friends. Each was going through a situation that involved other adults and in listening to the details, I decided that each situation was or could result in complete and total drama. My immediate response was, "***Don't get on the ride.***" I don't recall if they knew immediately what I meant when I said this, but for purposes of this conversation, please allow me to explain.

When I said, "Don't get on the ride," I meant do not get on someone else's emotional rollercoaster. Did any of the friends listen to me? One listened; the other didn't until later, but managed to survive the ride. Grace be to God!

Allow me to provide definitions for the words ***emotional*** and ***roller coaster.***

Emotional: Markedly aroused or agitated in feeling or sensibilities.

Roller Coaster: Marked by numerous ups and downs.

How ironic! Hence, an emotional rollercoaster could be defined as markedly aroused feelings characterized by numerous ups and downs. Is this you? Can anyone relate? How many times in life can you recall, wherein someone you know initiated a conversation with you that you knew was going to take you through multiple levels of emotions and in the end, you are left to wonder, "Why did I even go down this road?"

The better question is, "Why did I get on this ride"?

Side Note: I have deduced that some people like drama, and therefore would not benefit from reading this chapter. However, if you are a person who desires to live peaceable, whole lives with healthy relationships, read on.

---

[26]Mark 4:17

So assuming you have acknowledged that you are in fact guilty of stepping up to the ride, sitting down and strapping yourself in, I would like to offer you some advice. I will attempt to do this by asking you a series of questions, "therapy style," to assist you in achieving a more positive outcome, and thereby diminishing the number of rides you take from this point forward.

Why do you insist on riding other people's emotional roller coasters?

_____

_____

_____

_____

How do you end up on the roller coaster in the first place?

_____

_____

_____

_____

How can you get off of the ride once you've sat down, buckled up and are in motion?

_____

_____

_____

_____

How can you avoid taking this ride again, ever?

_____

_____

_____

_____

Bueller, anyone? I decided to check the Bible and see what the Lord says about emotional roller coasters. I know there were no roller coasters in the Bible, but there is evidence of emotional highs and lows.

In **Galatians 5:16-21 (MSG)**, the Lord says, *"My counsel is this: Live freely, animated and motivated by God's Spirit. Then you won't feed the compulsions of selfishness. For there is a root of sinful self-interest in us that is at odds with a free spirit, just as the free spirit is incompatible with selfishness. These two ways of life are antithetical, so that you cannot live at times one way and at times another way according to how you feel on any given day. Why don't you choose to be led by the Spirit and escape the erratic compulsions of a law-dominated existence? It is obvious what kind of life develops out of trying to get your own way all the time: repetitive, loveless, cheap sex; a stinking accumulation of mental and emotional garbage; frenzied and joyless grabs for happiness; trinket gods; magic-show religion; paranoid loneliness; cutthroat competition; all-consuming-yet-never-satisfied wants; a brutal temper; an impotence to love or be loved; divided homes and divided lives; small-minded and lopsided pursuits; the vicious habit of depersonalizing everyone into a rival; uncontrolled and uncontrollable addictions; ugly parodies of community."*

I could go on.

The Apostle Paul is telling us simply, to seek God, be led by the Holy Spirit when dealing with others and to love others as we love ourselves. If we would apply this simple, yet powerful solution, we would not take so many rides.

You may be asking yourself, "How can I apply this to my everyday life?" I'm so glad you asked:

1. **Proverbs 16:1(AMP)** said: *"The plans of the mind and orderly thinking belong to man, but from the Lord comes the (wise) answer of the tongue. In essence, pray before you speak and allow God to speak for you."*

2. **Proverbs 29:11 (ESV)** states: *"A fool gives full vent to his spirit, but a wise man **quietly** holds it back."* Maintain a 'military silence'. In other words, "just stop talking." I don't mean in the immature way of ignoring people and not speaking, I mean know when to listen and know when to speak.

3. **Romans 12:20 (ESV)** states, *"If your enemy is hungry, feed him; if he is thirsty, give him something to drink; for by so doing you will **heap** burning **coals** on his head."* Coal is used in the Bible to kill germs and burn off corruption. Isn't that powerful?! If you are kind to someone there is no way they can continue on with negativity.

4. **Psalm 34:14 (KJ21)** said: *"Depart from evil and do good; **seek peace** and **pursue** it."* Some of us may be adding to the perpetual state of riding. If this is the case, stop immediately and decide that you want peace, you have peace and you're going to keep the peace!

I pray this Word has helped someone to remove their seat belt and proceed to the exit gate determined to ride no more! Please consider the Word of God and use wisdom the next time someone invites you to take an emotional rollercoaster ride and you will be much better off.

"C" Is For The Chastening Rod

The first thing you need to understand is C=L.

No, this is not an advanced mathematical equation. It is the truth, Chastening = Love.

According to **Hebrews 12:6,** God chastises them that He loves.

God also reinforces this again in **Revelation 3:19 (ISV)**, *"I correct and discipline those whom I love, so be serious and repent!"*

When God begins the chastening process, we see Him as mean and unloving. This is the selfish response of a wayward child, because this is the same response we gave to our parents when we were younger. Isn't it time we grow up and accept that we can't just go through life, especially as a Christian, doing whatever we want, when we want, using our freedom in Christ as a means to continue sinning? As the Apostle Paul said, "god forbid"!

I had the privilege of attending a sermon some years ago and the preacher was teaching in part on the rod and staff of God. He explained that the staff was used to guide the sheep and the rod was used to break the legs of sheep, which constantly wandered off. Wow! Well, I wanted to check it out for myself.

In looking to Merriam-Webster, I found that the rod is also synonymous with punishment or suffering, pain, or loss that serves as retribution or a penalty inflicted on an offender through judicial procedure. Basically, when we step out of line, he whacks us with the rod and we deserve it. And not because He's mean but because He's just. There is a process of examining right from wrong and assigning blame.

Do you believe that? Yes____ No___

Next, I look up the word "staff."

Staff: A long stick used for support and also as a symbol of office or authority.

So, what does this mean? God uses His staff to support us and to lead us and He has the authority to do so. Additionally, if you study the scriptures to see instances where the staff is used; you will understand that the staff has power when wielded by God.

Do you respect His authority or do you resent it?

There are oftentimes when as children of God, we displease God in some way or we fall into sin. God can and will use these times to teach us through chastening. It doesn't feel good, but it is for our good and for His glory.

There is more that I could say here; however, the Word speaks for itself.

Why Are You Settling For Less?

When we put our hope and faith in what we see, we are potentially settling for less. As I was writing this, I was writing from the perspective of someone who always settled for less in people, especially men. However, I realized that my life involved a pattern of settling for less from myself, in school, finances and with opportunities where I played it safe instead of trying for more.

Through the power and the Word of God, I have been set free and I know that for the believer, there is NO limit. The Lord tells us in **Luke 12:32** to fear not, little flock, for our Father has been pleased to give us the kingdom.

Kingdom: The eternal kingship of God, the realm in which God's will is fulfilled and an area or sphere in which one holds a preeminent [paramount rank, dignity or importance].

This means that God has given us (all of us) a place, whereby His will is performed and He has given us top rank.

If this is the case, then why do we choose the bottom ranks in our life?

We know His Word is true; therefore, the problem is really us. We make the choice to not believe or act on what we know as the Word and the will of God for our life.

Let's take a look at the four lepers in **2 Kings 7.** Take a moment to read it now. It will bless you.

In this scripture, the lepers had a choice to make - life or death; belief or doubt. What will you decide?

I am willing to take a chance and 'go outside the gate.' I could have stayed in all of the places I found myself in; lonely, starving (figuratively speaking), lost; or I could take a chance. The lepers took a chance and found food, provision and wealth and as a result of the love in their hearts, they went back and let their other friends and family know.

This is what I want to do for you. I went outside the gates of bondage, sin, depression, lack, fear… you know the story. I found God's abundant provision in the areas of food, finances and love and now I want to share it with you.

Part of this knowledge involves a Kingdom mindset. We are not simply striving to be free here on earth. We are striving heavenward. Our true home is with God in His eternal kingdom. So as we live, we must live in a way that exemplifies this fact and therefore, allows us to never settle for less in how we act, live, love, talk, think and walk.

Will you come outside of the gates you have set up in your thinking and take a chance?

Yes____ No____ If no, then when? ____

In what areas of your life are you settling for less? What are you going to do about it?

_____

_____

_____

What Is That Smell?

There are times in our life that we find ourselves in situations where we really need help. Yet, we won't ask or seek God for it. Instead we look to outside means or even self-reliance to get us through.

I was led to read **Isaiah 65** while preparing this. What the Lord was saying through the prophet Isaiah was that He was waiting for someone to cry out to Him and ask Him for help. But instead, the children of Israel rebelled and sought help by worshipping idols and being hypocritical. God said that the people were a stench in His nostrils, an acrid (bitter, harsh and corrosive) smell that never went away.

Do you have any idols in your life that you seek out prior to seeking God? Before you respond, read the definition of an "idol":

Idol: An image or other material object representing a deity to which religious worship is addressed or any person or thing regarded with blind admiration, adoration, or devotion.

Who is the first person, place or thing, other than God, that you go to when you need help? _____

Many times, we seek answers within ourselves and reason within ourselves regarding our situations and choices. I don't mean the quiet introspection of seeking to hear from the Holy Spirit, I mean the heart that decides, "I know what's best for me, and I have this figured out."

92

This is a form of pride and this is an abomination to God.[27]

I just have one question: If God could smell you, would you be a sweet smell, or would you be an acrid smell?

Based on your response, hear what God is saying:

If you continue to take your own way, God will repay you in the same measure; however, assuming you responded truthfully, there is hope. God says humble yourself under His mighty hand and He will exalt you in due season.[28] Also, He will leave a remnant of those who heeded His voice and turned from their wickedness, and He will bless them.[29]

---

[27] Proverbs 6:16
[28] 1 Peter 5:6
[29] Isaiah 65

Transformative Thinking

Transformative: To change in character or condition.

Romans 12:2 (NIV) tells us not to conform to the pattern of this world, but be transformed by the renewing of your mind. Then you will be able to test and approve what God's will is - His good, pleasing and perfect will for your life.

Do you want to be transformed? Do you want to change? Yes___ No__ .

Write down some of the areas (in your mind) that you need or want transformed:

_____

_____

_____

_____

Do you keep doing the same things over and over again and expecting a different result? Will you choose to be brave enough to take a stand for holiness and righteousness and thereby receive a truly different experience?

There are times when we are no better than the children of Israel were - complaining, wandering around lost, confrontational, depressed and mentally enslaved. As we have learned, their freedom was seemingly no more important to them than a plate of food and comfortableness.

Isn't that really the issue?

You are comfortable where you are and the thought of actually changing is too burdensome, uncomfortable and scary. Therefore, the known facts are easier to deal with then delving into the unknown. This means, beloved that you are in bondage and unable or unwilling to break out. But breakout you must.

I heard a sermon a while ago that referenced the process of "being transformed by the renewing of your mind." The Pastor said that transformation and renewal have the implication of moving or rearranging furniture.

Are you prepared to move remodel or rearrange your thoughts? Yes____ No____

What are three things; mindsets, behaviors, relationships or issues that you could change right now that could transform your life into the one that God has for you?

_____

_____

_____

Read and Meditate on these scriptures:

1.	Jeremiah 33:3	Great and wondrous things
2.	2 Timothy 1:7	Fear
3.	Joshua 1:9	Courage
4.	2 Corinthians 12:9	Strength
5.	Proverbs 28:1	Boldness
6.	Joel 2:13	Change
7.	Romans 12:2	Transform

List the steps you can take to transform your mind:

_____

_____

_____

Do Step One now…and then Step Two and so on.

"So do not fear, for I am with you; do not be dismayed, for I am your God. I will strengthen you and help you; I will uphold you with my righteous right hand." **Isaiah 41:10 (NIV)**

"I can do ALL things through Christ which strengtheneth me. Philippians 4:13(KJV)

Get Rid Of The Clutter

The Bible tells us in **Luke 12:15** to beware of covetousness and seeking after things, for one's life does not consist in the abundance of things he possesses. We are encouraged rather to seek God first. [30]

Clutter: To run in disorder and to fill or cover with scattered or disordered things that impede movement or reduce effectiveness.

Time and again, God has used me to give a Word to a brother or sister that involved them cleaning house. By cleaning house, God meant a number of different things depending upon the circumstances or person intended.

Some of us need to clean house **physically**, meaning our actual home is beginning to become overrun with disorganization - piles of laundry, piles of papers, piles of trash, and piles of just stuff. Or we have collected things over the years that we just don't want to part with. I can

---

[30] Matthew 6:33

tell you that unless you let some things go, you cannot grab hold to the new things God wants to give you.

Others of us are cluttered in our **mind**. We simply cannot think straight because our environment is cluttered or we just have so much going on, we don't have one clear thought.

Then there is the **emotional** clutter, where we are so filled with emotions that we are just ruled by them. We can go from zero to 60 towards happy, mad, sad, glad and back again within minutes.

Lastly, the area of our life that suffers the most is your **Spirit** man. He is choked from being underneath and surrounded by all of this clutter. God is speaking, but you can't hear because of all of the clutter. You have got to clean this mess up! I was lamenting to a friend of mine about the fact that I could never hear God. She said, "He is always speaking; we fail to listen."

I remember a speaker some years ago who was talking about how he and his son were packing for a trip. He was in a store picking up things that he didn't necessarily need to take on that trip, and his son said, "Put those back. They are not a part of your destiny. You won't need that for where you are going."

Let's take a moment to revisit the SUPERb Woman Supply List:

Uniforms: The belt of truth; breastplate of righteousness; shoes of readiness fitted form the gospel of peace; the shield of faith; the helmet of salvation and the sword of the Spirit, which is the word of God.

Food/Provision: Man shall not live by bread alone, but by every word that proceeds out of the mouth of God.

*Shovel: B*ecause you are going to have to dig your way out of some places.

A good attitude: Some of you are going to have trouble here because things will get tough.

Map: The steps of a good man are ordered by the Lord and He delighteth in his way.

Water: Jesus is the living water. The Holy Spirit (our help and comforter)

Prayer journal: Your prayer journal is located at the end of this book. You will need to read it daily as your 'daily bread' for sustenance on this journey home.

Notebook: So that you can take orders, as they come, and remember pertinent facts, changes and occurrences.

Do you need these things for the journey you are on?

Yes_____No_____

Time To Declutter!

Honesty is the best policy so please, no excuses or putting things off. This has gone on LONG enough!

Phase 1: Assess the Clutter

<u>**Physical**</u>

Is my home cluttered? If yes, then why do you have so much clutter? And what will you do today to start the process of de-cluttering?" Is any of this stuff (i.e. people, places or things) in God's will for my life or necessary for where I am going?

_____

_____

_____

_____

<u>**Mental**</u>

What is on my mind? What things can I control? What things do I have no control over? Will I give them to God? How do I do that? Are these thoughts of God? Are these thoughts pleasing to God or necessary for the path God would have me to walk?

_____

_____

_____

_____

_____

<u>**Emotional**</u>

Why are my nerves so frazzled? Why does EVERYTHING make me emotional? What can I do to not feel this way anymore? How do I get my emotions under control? Are God's emotions and behaviors all over the place like this?

_____

_____

_____

_____

Spiritual

Is my Spirit man alive and active or does he need mouth-to-mouth resuscitation? How do I reconnect with the Holy Spirit?

_____

_____

_____

_____

In writing this, I was reminded of the rich man who made a lot of money and his barns were full and he said to himself, 'I will build a bigger barn to hold my stuff,' and God said to him, *"You fool tonight, your soul is required of you."*

So with all of the hoarding of money and things, he died and it was just left there. Just think, what could you do if you were free and clear in your body, mind, emotions and spirit? You could bless and be blessed!

Phase II: Take these steps

Physically: Decide that you will have a yard sale, a donation drop-off or giveaway day to family, friends and neighbors. Just get rid of that stuff! *"Watch out! Be on your guard against all kinds of greed; a man's life does not consist in the abundance of his possessions."* **Luke 12:15 (NIV)**

Mentally: Ask the Lord to cleanse your mind and let go of the past or those things you have no control over. *"Therefore, if anyone is in Christ, he is a new creation; the old has gone, the new has come!"* **2 Corinthians 5:17 (NIV)**

Emotionally: *"Think on those things that are true, honorable, right, pure, lovely and admirable. Do not be anxious about anything, but in everything, by prayer and petition, with thanksgiving, present your requests to God.* **"Philippians 4:6 (NIV)**

Spiritually: Ask the Lord to forgive you for placing things before Him and to cleanse your heart and mind so that you can hear His voice. Then be still and listen. *"Create in me a pure heart, O God, and renew a steadfast spirit within me."* **Psalm 51 (NIV)**

De-Cluttering Isn't Easy

De-cluttering isn't easy; however, it is MANDATORY. On the next leg of your journey, you will be living in cramped quarters; and, there will be NO room for all of this junk! In addition, you are going to have to make some changes and now is the time for you to pull over and get a makeover. You can't go home looking like you look right now.

Worm Juice

I know the title is compelling right? I mean, *worm juice*?! Obviously, it worked because here you are reading it. I have been on a journey, for some time. I think that, as dumb as this sounds, this has only just become clear to me. This leg of the trip involves a swimming phase and a resting phase - legs not required, drowning possible.

My husband, who is just the "best" traveling companion, and I were traveling, this past December to Georgia to pick up our son. During the trip, we took the time to listen to an audio teaching series by a popular televangelist. I don't recall the title of the series we listened to, however, I distinctly remember one particular aspect of the message she shared that spoke to me. She spoke on the process of growing from a caterpillar to a butterfly. She said it must be really nasty in the cocoon phase, because God never lets us see what's going on in the cocoon. I thought to myself, this is SO true! We see the caterpillar spin the cocoon, and then we see the cocoons hanging in the trees and then poof! One day, they're empty and you see lots and lots of really beautiful butterflies.

The televangelist went on to say, "I decided that in the cocoon, there must be a lot of muck and juice and just icky stuff going on." I could *totally* relate! I turned to my husband and I said, "You know what? She is describing me, I feel like *"worm juice."* For a long time I have not been clear at all as to where I'm going, or even who I am at this point. I can't pinpoint where this started. I know that I'm a wife, mother, daughter, sister, friend (not always a good one). Please forgive me, people), a Christian, business owner and a doctor of business! But what does that all mean?

I hope you're still with me on this…

In October of 2008, I clearly heard the Lord say, *"Cut your hair and take off those fake nails."*

Okay Lord, done!

In May 2009, I heard the Lord say, *"Set yourself free. You're clear to leave your job."* Okay Lord, done!

He told me to build my house. Okay, I think I got it. . . thought I had it . . .

Nope, I got nothing.

I began building the way I thought He meant me to build, with my physical fitness (definitely not there yet); being a better wife and mom (still in the process); ministering to people, being a motivational speaker, and growing my business. He gave me lots of ideas, and I wrote them all down, he even gave me this book to write. Then one day, it all stopped! Did I stop? Did He stop?

Toto, I don't think we're in Kansas anymore…

As you can imagine, this sent me into somewhat of a tailspin as I'm a person who *always* had to have the answer for everything – Okay, I still do at times! I want to know ALL of the details and what's coming next. Well, I didn't clearly have an answer yet, and I knew that I could call any one of my many friends, colleagues, parents or family members for a lengthy discourse on what I should, could or might be doing. However, the only thing I was sure of is, when you're in the worm juice, it stinks. It's dark, you can't see, it's scary and it's hard to hear. It's also *very* cramped. I wanted to get out, but my wings just weren't strong enough yet. I wonder if anyone else can relate?

I had all sorts of thoughts inside the worm juice, *"God, are you listening? Are you still there? I can't hear you! Have you forgotten about me? Did I do something wrong? I'm ready to go! When is my turn coming? Have I missed you? When is this going to end? Okay, whatever, I'll be still…"*

So, normally, I would give a step-by-step process for getting out of this place. But I realize that the only way out is to wait until it's time to come out and that all time belongs to God. Some of you may not be in this place or have already come out. If you are in it, then be encouraged that you are NOT alone. If you are already out, PRAISES BE TO GOD! I bet your wings are strong and you are *beautiful.* Please pray for others to make it out, too!

*In this phase, I didn't desire advice, as there are places we go in life that ONLY God can reach us; however, I did ask for prayer - prayer that I would continue to be still, that I would be strong and that I would hear His voice. More importantly, I wanted them to pray that I would come out ready to fly *in due season.*

The View From The Juice

My husband and I were at dinner one evening discussing my chapter on *worm juice*. We were discussing how this phase had been for him. Although he was not necessarily in the juice with me, he had to come along for the ride since he said, "I do."

Specifically, we were discussing that in this state a woman, or even the man going through it, is:

- Not as attractive;

- Might act "stank" – often;

- Might not be at their best all the way around;

- Has no idea when this is going to end;

- Cannot receive outside assistance.

We both felt as though this discussion was relevant because unless your spouse understands what phases you are in - spiritually, mentally, physically, and emotionally - they cannot adapt to the situation in a wise way and may be put off by the transformations taking place in your life. Bless their little hearts… This in turn, can lead to problems in the relationship and create room for the enemy to move in.

I asked my husband to give me a male point of view and also to check his pulse, since he was in the worm juice with me! His response was **Ephesians 5:25-28 (MSG)**. I decided to share the Message Version as I thought it really brought the point home:

"Husbands, go all out in your love for your wives, exactly as Christ did for the church—a love marked by giving, not getting. Christ's love makes the church whole. His words evoke her beauty. Everything he does and says is designed to bring the best out of her, dressing her in dazzling white silk, radiant with holiness. And that is how husbands ought to love their wives. They're really doing themselves a favor—since they're already 'one' in marriage."

Isn't that awesome? He's definitely a keeper! I was in the worm juice feeling like a *total hot mess*, but God's whole job was to evoke my beauty! Thank you Jesus! What the scripture is really saying is that they're stuck with us, so they might as well make the best of it!

Just kidding!

Side Note: My husband reminded me (a little too enthusiastically) to add, "*As wives we must submit; if you are single, submit to God.*" This is in **Ephesians 5:24** and I totally agree. This is key, people, because not only must we submit to the process of going through the worm juice, but we must submit to what God is doing in and through us. And we must submit to our husbands in the same manner that we submit to God.

I know some of you just stopped reading right here; It'll be all right. Take a deep breath and come back.

He also mentioned that we should look at the characteristics of the Proverbs 31 woman's husband. Although the Bible doesn't expound on him, **Proverbs 31:23 (MSG)** states, *"Her husband is known in the gates when he sits among the elders of the land."*

Gate: Entering into; domination; dominion; power of authority; righteousness; heaven; salvation; thanksgiving; entering the presence of God; gates open up to: cities; prisons; sanctuaries; graves.(Strong's Concordance)

This is powerful as it implies that your husband is in authority as is his God-given right and that he can lead us into many different places, good or bad. And he is the gate to God for you.

Take a moment to study some of these scriptures: Write down the key message you receive from reading these.

Genesis 19: 1; 22: 17; 24:60

_____

_____

Hosea 2:15

_____

_____

Exodus 32: 26-27

_____

_____

Hebrews 13: 12

_____

_____

1 Corinthians 16: 9

_____

_____

2 Corinthians 2: 12

_____

_____

Colossians 4:3

_____

_____

Matthew 16: 18

_____

_____

John 10: 7, 9

_____

_____

Revelation 4:1; 3:8, 20

_____

_____

Psalms 24:7; 100:4; 107:16; 122:2; 141:3

_____

_____

This verse also references **Proverbs 12:4 (MSG)** which states, _"A hearty wife invigorates her husband, but a frigid woman is cancer in the bones."_

Hearty: Giving unqualified support, enthusiastically or exuberantly cordial.

Cancer: Something evil or malignant that spreads destructively.

In other words, don't let the worm juice go to your head. Keep a good attitude while going through this process and everyone will make it out alive!

Clue: BE HEARTY.

What are your thoughts?

_____

_____

_____

_____

*Warning: a major area of concern on this journey is "wheel spinning."

Don't Talk About It, Be About It

I find people who are always talking about what they're going to do but never doing anything to be extremely frustrating. Each time you see them, they are still talking about what they are going to do.

Now there are a number of reasons, such as fear, why forward motion never takes place, apathy, laziness, confusion, (**You fill in the blank**). Please note: None of these reasons are characteristic of who God is and none of them are a fruit of the spirit, according to **Galatians 5.** The Proverbs 31 sister was a doer.

Proverbs 31:13-31 KJV tells us: *"She seeketh wool, and flax, and worketh willingly with her hands. She is like the merchants' ships; she bringeth her food from afar. She riseth also while it is yet night, and giveth meat to her household, and a portion to her maidens. She considereth a field, and buyeth it: with the fruit of her hands she planteth a vineyard. She girdeth her loins with strength, and strengtheneth her arms. She perceiveth that her merchandise is good: her candle goeth not out by night. She layeth her hands to the spindle, and her hands hold the distaff. She stretcheth out her hand to the poor; yea, she reacheth forth her hands to the needy. She is not afraid of the snow for her household: for all her household are clothed with scarlet. She maketh herself coverings of tapestry; her clothing is silk and purple. Her husband is known in the gates, when he sitteth among the elders of the land. She maketh fine linen, and selleth it; and delivereth girdles unto the merchant. Strength and honour are her clothing; and she shall rejoice in time to come. She openeth her mouth with wisdom; and in her tongue is the law of kindness. She looketh well to the ways of her household, and eateth not the bread of idleness. Her children arise up, and call her blessed; her husband also, and he praiseth her. Many daughters have done virtuously, but thou excellest them all. Favour is deceitful, and beauty is vain: but a woman that feareth the LORD, she shall be praised. Give her of the fruit of her hands; and let her own works praise her in the gates."*

I can just hear you saying, "I know she is not suggesting that I do all of these things in the midst of all that I already do!" Surely not. However, my suggestion is that you take inventory of where you are and what you are doing to determine if your inventory lines up with the will of God and the "things" the Proverbs 31 woman did. As we see from the Word, her activities were pleasing to God and she found favor.

Is your life pleasing to God? Do you have favor with Him and others?

_____

_____

_____

_____

_____

In addition, there isn't any portion of this scripture that reference her sitting around talking about what she was going to do. She simply handled her business. She didn't ask people what they thought she should do. Her husband trusted her decisions and she prospered. (*Proverbs 31:26 She speaks with wisdom, and faithful instruction is on her tongue.*)

Back to you - What have you talked about and talked about and never gotten around to doing? This is the thing you would do if money were no object, if you didn't have to take care of the kids, if your husband was more supportive, or if you weren't afraid, lazy, apathetic, confused, (**YOU fill in the blanks**).

_____

_____

_____

What am I always talking about doing?

_____

_____

_____

_____

What or who has actually gotten in my way?

_____

_____

Now, this next step is going to take some unbelievable audacity or chutzpa on your part. You have determined what the "thing" is, and what's blocking your ability to do it. Now it's time for you to take some action to "get 'er done".

No More Excuses

The Proverbs 31 sister made it happen and she had all of the same responsibilities we have. Oftentimes we give advice and tell people what they should do, but we never provide a roadmap by which they can operate. Therefore, let me help you out:

STEP 1: PUT GOD FIRST

We have discussed the importance of putting Christ first, front and center. Be sure to read **Matthew 6:33** again. If you don't believe me, read **Luke 10:40-42**. In this particular story, Jesus has been invited to have dinner with Martha, Mary and others. Martha was concerned with dinner preparations whereas Mary spent her time visiting with Jesus. Martha became frustrated at Mary for not helping her and asked Jesus to make Mary help. Jesus told Martha, *"You are too concerned about too many things; Mary has chosen the good thing."*

Recommit yourself to Him and remove Him from the passenger seat, backseat or trunk of your life. In order for this to work, He has to be first. **Take a moment to repent and recommit your life to Christ.**

Prayer: *Father, in the name of Jesus, I repent for allowing daily and life distractions to take your place in my life and I ask your forgiveness now, in Jesus' name. I recommit myself to you and ask that you take your rightful place as the head of my life and my family's life; and in accordance with Proverbs 3:5-6. I release, leaning to my own understanding, and I acknowledge you in every area of my life. I ask that You direct my paths from this point forward, in Jesus' holy and precious name. Amen.*

STEP 2: DETERMINE THE STEPS YOU NEED TO TAKE TO MAKE THIS "THING" A REALITY

Don't get caught up focusing on fear in lack of finances. **2 Corinthians 9:10 (NIV)** tells us, *"Now he who supplies seed to the sower and bread for food will also supply and increase your store of seed and will enlarge the harvest of your righteousness."*

Write down the steps you'll need to take:

_____

_____

_____

_____

_____

STEP 3: DETERMINE WHO CAN HELP BRING YOUR DREAM TO LIFE

Ask God to show you who He has assigned to help you.

Make a list:

_____

_____

_____

_____

* Don't tell everyone - Ask God who you should share your vision with as everyone will not be supportive. Use wisdom. _"Look, I am sending you out as sheep among wolves. So be as shrewd as snakes and harmless as doves._ **"Matthew 10:16 (NLT)**

STEP 4: DETERMINE A TIMELINE. What is your goal date for getting this 'thing' done? (**Proverbs 29:18 (NIV):** _"Where there is no revelation, people cast off restraint; but blessed is the one who heeds wisdom's instruction."_)

_____

_____

_____

_____.

STEP 5: WORK YOUR PLAN, ONE STEP AT A TIME.

As you complete a task, mark it out and go to the next one.

Write down your first step and do it.

_____

_____

_____

STEP 6: REMEMBER GOD AND KNOW THAT GOD GIVES US THE ABILITY TO BUILD WEALTH

Deuteronomy 8:18 (KJV) states: _"But thou shalt remember the LORD thy God: for [it is] he that giveth thee power to get wealth, that he may establish his covenant which he swore unto thy fathers, as [it is] this day."_

STEP 7: SHUT UP! DON'T SAY ANOTHER WORD! FROM THIS POINT FORWARD, THE ONLY ACTION IS ACTION.

Purpose in your heart that you will be a person of action and that you will no longer waste your time, or others' time, talking about what you're going to do.

Read **James 2:14-17 (MSG)**: *"Dear friends, do you think you'll get anywhere in this if you learn all the right words but never do anything? Does merely talking about faith indicate that a person really has it? For instance, you come upon an old friend dressed in rags and half-starved and say, 'Good morning, friend! Be clothed in Christ! Be filled with the Holy Spirit!' and walk off without providing so much as a coat or a cup of soup—where does that get you?*

Isn't it obvious that God-talk without God-acts is outrageous nonsense?"

In our culture, we live in a time where there is *so* much to do that it is practically overwhelming. But Jesus reminds us, as He did Martha, that the BEST thing to do is just rest at His feet and let Him teach us what to do. He would like for us to be like Mary, who chose to spend time with God as opposed to being occupied and busy with the things of the world. Please don't confuse "being occupied and busy with the things of the world" to mean that you don't have time to do the "thing" we are talking about. Part of your problem has been worldly distractions in the forms of all of the things you have to do.

Put God first and then focus on the "things" that God gave, gifted and blessed you to do and all things will come together for you. I am working this advice by writing this book and I believe that, "all other things will be added" unto me, once I finish it, in Jesus' name!

Don't talk about it, BE ABOUT IT!

Please, Stand Still…Just Stop!

I know that it is not proper to start a sentence with a question, but have you ever wanted something so bad that you could hardly wait? Or has God gave you a vision and you said, "Yes", and began moving in the direction you were led in, believing for the end? Or is your dream so close you can see it, but you can't get to it?

Writing this book involved a series of waiting periods and waiting room experiences. Do you know what I mean? The waiting period involves just that, waiting for something to happen next so you know which direction to take. The waiting room period is like waiting and waiting and not knowing what the outcome is going to be – life, death, somewhere in between?

God allowed me to be tested by a number of situations. Prior to writing this chapter, the Lord sent Word through His prophet for me to get this book finished. I had been waiting and He was stretching me during this waiting, but now it's time and I need to write! There are promises tied to this book and so much more.

"Then the LORD *answered me, "Write the vision. Make it clear on tablets so that anyone can read it quickly. The vision will still happen at the appointed time. It hurries toward its goal. It won't be a lie. If it's delayed, wait for it. It will certainly happen. It won't be late."* **Habakkuk 2:2-3 (GW)**

Praise God!

I believe the Holy Spirit was speaking to me as He did to Nehemiah and Haggai that God has called me to rebuild His people and His temple – and are we not His temple? And in the midst of this writing (rebuilding) opposition will and has come. However, I am encouraged and pray that you are as well.

Read Nehemiah 1-10 and Haggai 1-7.

As soon as Nehemiah began the process of rebuilding, he came under attack of fear, persecution and even the threat of physical harm. In the book of Haggai, the Lord admonishes the people for their laziness and greed in building their own homes, while His temple lies in ruins. He goes on to tell them that they will no longer profit from their work or deeds until His temple has been restored.

Do you understand this?

In the midst of writing this book, I have been offered full-time employment, side gigs and other jobs. People from my past, who I am certain mean no good, have attempted to contact me. My back aches; I am tired; money is tight and on and on. Yet one thing remains constant in my mind: I must complete the work that God has given me so that none of those he has assigned to me is lost and all is restored, as He intended.

We have, throughout this journey, discussed the many visions, dreams, abilities and callings God has placed on your life. You must know that as He begins to peel you away from your jobs, your stuff, your desires to turn your face towards Him, you will come under attack, from within and from without, but you MUST commit to finishing the task He has placed before you.

God has shown me the vision. What is the vision He has shown you?

_____

_____

_____

_____

The interesting thing about God is He will show us a portion of the vision, and we say, "yes," without reading the fine print. He rarely shows us the middle portion, and therefore, all we have to go on is the vision - the end result. The middle portion - or the middle place, if you will - is where the testing, trials, attacks and faith kick in.

The middle place is where we begin to doubt and become fearful and confused. These are not characteristics of God. We forget the vision or begin to wonder if we heard correctly. We may begin to seek counsel from others about what to do and where we are going.

I Beg You, Please Stand Still! Just Stop!

First of all, God gave the vision to you, meaning only you can see it. Secondly, the minute we begin to seek others, we take our eyes off of God and the vision He has given us. Therefore, doubt and confusion enter in.

You have come to this place many times, and as a result, have never completed the course. You must stand still, stop speaking, stop seeking and don't do *anything* until you hear from God.

*Begin a fast for three days and commit to only speak to and hear from God. The purpose is to cleanse out your spirit man and prepare to hear from God.

In the middle place, you will have to use your supplies. I pray you brought them with you. This is a place of testing and therefore, equipment is essential and prior preparation is mandatory. In this place, many people forget who they are and they begin to doubt who God is.

(No worries, God ALWAYS knows whose we are and where we are.) Check your equipment and ensure you have the following on hand:

- Helmet of Salvation
- Sword of the Spirit - Word of God
- Shield of Faith
- Breastplate of Righteousness - in place
- Belt of Truth- buckled around your waist
- Feet shed with the preparation of the Gospel of Peace
- Always pray in the Spirit

Instructions

We will assume you are already saved because we took care of this in the beginning. Furthermore, an unsaved person would not be on this journey. You must know the Word of God (i.e. the vision for your life) so that you can overcome any confusion and doubt. This is to be used as your map and compass.

God's Word, in **Jeremiah 29:11 (NIV)** states, *"'For I know the plans I have for you,' declares the LORD, 'plans to prosper you and not to harm you, plans to give you hope and a future.'"*

• The **Shield of Faith** must be held up at all times, because without it, you will not please God; and without it, you will not believe God.

• The **Breastplate of Righteousness** must be worn over your heart at ALL times. With the heart, we believe unto righteousness; your heart must remain pure and devoted to the task for which God has called you to. Your heart is the guide and the mechanism by which God can speak to you. Keep it open to Him only and guard it well.

• The **Belt of Truth** is critical, as without the truth, you will not be free; prepare your feet to walk in peace. Peace is a fruit of the spirit and we are told that God will keep them in perfect peace whose mind is stayed on Him. Keep focused on Him and He will order your steps. If you cannot hear Him or He is not speaking, then your feet should be still and in preparation to move.

• Lastly, seek God through His Spirit, speaking to Him in prayer (worship Him in spirit and in truth) and WAIT for His response. For in the end, His Word shall speak and not lie.

I believe, wholeheartedly, that in the midst of your fast, God will show you any hindrance and issues. Upon completion of your fast, God will have revealed to you what your next step is. Once God has spoken, take the step.

"My sheep hear My voice, and I know them, and they follow Me." **John 10:27 (KJV)**

What steps has He directed you to take?

_____

_____

_____

_____

"I will instruct thee and teach thee in the way which thou shalt go: I will guide thee with mine eye." **Psalm 32:8 (KJV)**

If in the end of the fast, He has yet to speak, continue to be still - prepare your feet - and believe God.

What should you do while you wait? Psalm 27:14 and Isaiah 40:31 will guide you:

_____

_____

_____

Standing still or being still does NOT come easy to many people. I know it surely was nearly impossible for me to be still. I believe this is because we are free will beings and inherently self-sufficient. Many of us are doers, planners and impatient.

Can you relate?

In any case, throughout a series of guided mishaps and pitfalls (all ordained by God), I have learned the importance and necessity of being still. I know beyond a shadow of a doubt that obedience is _much_ better than the sacrifice you will have to make for moving forward apart from God's will.

What have you learned and discovered while waiting?

_____

_____

_____

_____

_____

What God Has For You, is For You

I struggled to figure out how God wanted me to write this chapter. I didn't struggle from lack of what to say as much as how to say it and wanting to get it right. There are so many ways to address this section.

Why do I say this? Thank you for asking! I will give you a couple scenarios:

1. Caren is in school and is working towards a PhD. Caren is incredibly brilliant and is one of the most intelligent, well-spoken women I know. Notwithstanding, she is a mom, wife, a Christian and hysterically funny. She has taken more than seven years to complete her PhD, because she is afraid that she is inadequate and is convinced that what she has to say is not relevant. God has designed her degree to become a program that will set African-American families free.

What?!

114

The fact that she continues to get sidetracked in this process of completing her degree is a trick of the enemy to keep her pressed down and looking inward so that she never looks to the hills from which cometh her help. She never lives out the words, "I can do ALL things through Christ who strengthens me." Worse still, she could fail to accomplish the task God has given her which is to lead other families out of the wilderness and into what God has for them.[31]

My Lord!

Is this you? _____

2. Ashley is a hater. I mean she always hates and *rarely* congratulates, unless it's someone she deems is on her level and has made a lateral progression and not a vertical progression, which would cause HATERATION to arise. You know this person, as she is characterized as good looking, intelligent, well spoken, and etc., But because she fails to see herself in this way, she is always looking outward at what others have achieved, look like, have and do, and she inwardly hates herself for not having the same. Instead of using others as a catalyst, mentor and encouragement to go forward to greatness, she hates others and is *jealous and envious.* This greatly displeases God. If this is you, please admit it now.

Is this you? _____

In each scenario above, Caren and Ashley were more concerned with what others had and esteemed them higher than their individual selves.

This is characteristic of covetousness.

Let's look at what God says about us:

- **Psalm 139** tells us that, *"We are fearfully and wonderfully made."* And according to **Jeremiah 29:11** states: He knows the thoughts and plans that he has for us, says the Lord, thoughts and plans for welfare and peace and not for evil, to give us hope in our final outcome.

- God also tells us that a cattle on a thousand hills belong to Him[32] and that *"His desire is that we, as His beloved, prosper and be in health even as our soul prospereth,"* according to **3 John 2**.

- He has purposed abundance, according to **John 10:10**. So why are we looking at anyone else, when looking to God brings all that we need?

[31] Isaiah 61
[32] Psalm 50:10

What does this mean for you?

_____

_____

_____

If you are looking at anyone or anything else other than God, it is evil or has the potential to become sin (i.e. jealousy, envy, hatred, deceit, covetousness, pride, strife) in your life.

Do you believe that? _____.

Luke 6:45 (NIV) tells us, *"A good man brings good things out of the good stored up in his heart, and an evil man brings evil things out of the evil stored up in his heart. For the mouth speaks what the heart is full of."*

How can you move forward from this? Deal with this now because you cannot go home in bondage.

1. **Repent**. You must acknowledge that these thoughts are not of God and as such represent sin in your heart.

2. **Ask God** to fill those places in you where you feel lack or less than. He is well able to heal you and to fill in all empty or broken places.

3. **Be healed**. If you will meditate on the Word (especially those scriptures above) day and night, they will take root in your heart and become life inside of you.

4. When covetous or jealous thoughts rise up in your mind, **cast them down** in the name of Jesus, and thank God for all He has blessed you with. In your prayer time, seek Him for your heart's desires. Know that according to His Word, *"Delight yourself in the Lord and He will give you the desires of your heart."* **Psalm 37:4 (NIV)**

Set Yourself Free!

Recently, the Lord laid it on my heart to call a friend of mine whom I've known for quite some time. What I know about her is she is a wife, mother, friend, sister, child of God. She is also a self-proclaimed procrastinator.

In the midst of the conversation, the Lord used me to help her see some areas in her life, including procrastination, where she was bound and needed to be set free. In the middle of the conversation, she said, "The Lord is making me tell all my little secrets."

I thought this was just hilarious and I told her in jest, "You will be the topic of my next chapter."

The same day, I was driving home from picking my son up from school, and we passed a local establishment that had a picture of a woman with her finger up to her mouth. Ironically, the name of the establishment had something to do with secrets. I immediately thought of the conversation I had just had with my friend and it struck me that people keep so many secrets. What I feel was revealed, however, is *people are not keeping secrets; the secrets are keeping the people.*

If you have a secret that you have held onto for years in fear that you would be found out, destroyed, embarrassed, hurt, or your life would fall apart and you would rather die than have it revealed, then you are not holding the secret.

The secret is holding you.

The situation is just baffling to me in the sense that my friend is a child of God and therefore knows that God knows everything, therefore, who is she really keeping the secret from? Sin can make us look so foolish. Second, if you are reading this and you have not accepted Jesus as your Lord and Savior, please know that it still applies to you, because God is the God of the entire universe whether you believe in Him or not.

I believe it is important to note, there are some things that people keep secret for fear of hurting others if the secret is revealed. To this I say, it is God's will that we all live a life of freedom and as such you deserve to be free.

Consider speaking to your Pastor or a family counselor for secrets that are deep-seated and may have a profound affect on the family.

Do not allow the fear of affecting others negatively seduce you into remaining silent and in bondage. Speak out now and let everyone have the opportunity to heal! Regardless, God knows *everything*. He is omniscient and omnipresent meaning He is ALWAYS present and knows everything and can heal everything.

I would like to take a moment to prove to you scripturally, the foolishness of keeping secrets from God:

- **Isaiah 29:15 (NIV)** says, *"Woe to those who go to great depths to hide their plans from the LORD, who do their work in darkness and think, "Who sees us? Who will know?"*

- **Psalm 44:20-21 (NIV)** says, *"If we had forgotten the name of our God or spread out our hands to a foreign god, would not God have discovered it, since he knows the secrets of the heart?"*

- **Psalm 90:8 (NIV)** says, *"You have set our iniquities before you, our secret sins in the light of your presence."*
- **Jeremiah 23:24 (NIV)** states: *"'Can anyone hide in secret places so that I cannot see him?' declares the LORD. 'Do not I fill heaven and earth?' declares the LORD."*

*Prayerfully read Psalm 32.

What secret sins do you need to lay before God now?

_____

_____

_____

_____

_____

*Read Proverbs 12:22 to find out what God's thoughts are towards those who lie:

- Pray **Psalm 51** and ask God to forgive you as well as release you from the bondage of these sins.
- Read **Galatians 5:1**
- Read **Romans 12:2**

Prayer: *Let us pray, in agreement, that from this point forward you will decide to live a life of truth and righteousness. Therefore, have no need to keep any more personal secrets or anyone else's' secrets, in Jesus' name. Amen!*

It's Not My Fault! It's My Past!

 * *The Lord gave my husband the vision for this chapter.*

We share many common threads, me as the writer, and you as the readers of this book. One such thread is, we all have a past and we all have a future. You cannot get to the future or fully enjoy it, until you have dealt with, made peace and reconciled the past, good, bad or indifferent.

So the first thing I will say to you is, <u>STOP</u> being a victim! This is not said to be harsh or minimize your pain. The purpose and the point of this is to get you to accept things the way they were and the way they are, deal with them, and then move on, so that you can be free. As long as you make an excuse for yourself by saying, "It's not my fault; it's my past!" (or some such variation), you will always perpetuate this cycle. It's time to stop now and move on!

What happened to you may not have been your fault or your responsibility; however, you have a responsibility to live a life of excellence NOW and move forward. It will be your fault if you don't. The past does not have to win; it is gone. Why then are you still looking at it and carrying it around with you like a pocketbook everywhere you go?

When I first became divorced, I would always say to people, "I'm divorced," "I committed adultery" or something close to it. I did that unknowingly. Subconsciously, I just felt so sick and guilty that I believe I just wanted to make myself pay and I needed to let everyone know how awful I was and how sorry I felt all at the same time. What a mess!

Bless my heart.

One night I went to a prayer meeting and I did it again, and the minister leading the prayer said, "You don't have to introduce yourself like that or say those things about yourself. You were forgiven when you asked, and now you have to forgive yourself." She will never know how her words set me free that night. I was not immediately healed, but I was on the path to healing. And today, I can say, I am truly free.

PRAISE GOD!

Now, back to you…

What part of your past do you continue to hold onto, relive daily or refuse to let go of?

_____

_____

_____

_____

122

Prayerfully read and pray aloud the following scriptures:

"You were taught, with regard to your former way of life, to put off your old self, which is being corrupted by its deceitful desires." **Ephesians 4:22 (NIV)**

"Do not lie to each other, since you have taken off your old self with its practices." **Colossians 3:9 (NIV)**

"For we know that our old self was crucified with him so that the body of sin might be done away with, that we should no longer be slaves to sin." **Romans 6:6 (NIV)**

The Word of God tells us that we don't have to even be bothered with our "old" selves or stuff anymore. Most importantly, God has completely forgotten about our mess. We are the ones who hold on. **Psalm 103:12 (NIV)** tells us, *"As far as the east is from the west, so far has he removed our transgressions from us."*

Purpose in your heart today to do the same.

I'll Make Your Mess A Message

I heard someone say the other day on a radio broadcast, "God will take your mess and make it a message."

Oh my goodness! That is SO true!

I want you to just think about this for a moment and then write down your initial thoughts on how God can take your mess and make it a message.

_____

_____

_____

This is so awesome! I say this because there are so many instances in the Bible where God took people who were in the messiest of places and turned their entire situation around and used it and them as a message. Let's look at a few:

• **Bathsheba:** This book is based on Bathsheba and the life she led prior to becoming the Proverbs 31 woman. She was an adulteress and somewhat an accessory to murder. However, God redeemed her and she has become an icon for Godly women to aspire to. Most importantly, Jesus is descended from the bloodline of David and therefore, she ties in with the chain of events leading to His birth.

- **The Samaritan woman at the well**[33]: When she first encountered Jesus, she was in the midst of living with a man and had been with six others. Jesus asked her was she married to the man she was currently with and she said, "No." She could have lied to Him, but instead she chose to be transparent. This is how *you* must be before God - TRANSPARENT.

Transparent: Free from pretense or deceit.

People sometimes lie out of fear -fear of judgment; fear of consequences. But our God tells us, the truth shall set us free! After her encounter with Jesus and accepting the 'living water,' He encouraged her to become an evangelist. The Word tells us that many believed on Jesus because of her testimony.

- **Paul the Apostle:** He became one of the greatest ministers, teachers and evangelists in the kingdom of God. However, before he became Paul, his name was Saul and he was a murderer of Christian people. But one day, God called his name and blinded his vision. Upon receiving prayer and restored sight, he was unstoppable in ministering the Word of God and converting sinners to Christ.

- **Peter:** He was Jesus' favorite disciple and claimed he would never deny Jesus. However, when he was tested in this, he failed and denied Jesus three times! After Jesus' resurrection, He forgave Peter and established him as the cornerstone of the church.

Are you getting it?

Now that you have the proof that God can and will take your mess and turn it into a message, let's work on you:

What mess do you need to tell or give to God?

_____

_____

_____

What mess are you in?

_____

_____

_____

_____

---

[33] John 4:1-42

What message do you have to share with others?

_____

_____

_____

Bathsheba shared with us the ways in which we could be godly women. The Samaritan woman at the well gave the message that you can be a whore and still receive salvation and forgiveness, and then be used by God to bring salvation to others. Paul's message was teaching people how to live for God and praising God through suffering even though he previously persecuted God. Peter's message was, you can deny Christ and He will forgive you and place you in position to tell thousands of His goodness.

What steps are you going to take to start sharing your message?

_____

_____

_____

Proof of the impact of not sharing your message: If Bathsheba had not shared her message, King Solomon would not know what to look for in a godly wife and neither would other men, past and present, who need direction in this regard. We, as women, would not have had a roadmap for the lifestyle and characteristics that please God.

The Bible tells us that many more came and gave their life to Christ, as a result of the Samaritan woman's testimony. What if she had kept silent? And if Paul and the other disciples had kept their mess and message to themselves, 3,000 people would not have given their lives to Christ.[34]

Finally, if Peter had kept his mess and his message to himself, the modern day church might not exist, and we might not know that we can be forgiven for the ultimate betrayal - denying Jesus.

*Please realize that this is not about you and that God has allowed your mess to bring a message of the good news of Jesus Christ! Stop wallowing and cowering in fear, shame, doubt, self-pity, and get busy letting God clean up your mess.

Now, let Him use you to share your message.

---

[34] Acts 2:40

March To The Beat Of God's Drum: Dance to your own rhythm

There is an old adage that says, "March to the beat of your own drum." The word "march" in this instance is used to imply following after one's own heart and individuality, which I am all for. However, in this life the one beat we must learn to march to is God's.

The Holy Spirit led me to tell you to march to the beat of God's drum and dance to the rhythm of His grace. **1 Kings 8:56 (MSG)** confirms this: *"Blessed be GOD, who has given peace to his people Israel just as He said He would do."*

Not one of all those good and wonderful words that He spoke through Moses misfired. May GOD, our very own God, continue to be with us just as he was with our ancestors. May He never give up and walk out on us. May He keep us centered and devoted to him, following the life path He has cleared, watching the signposts and *walking at the pace and rhythms he laid down for our ancestors.*

Deuteronomy 12:10 (MSG) says, *"Don't continue doing things the way we're doing them at present, each of us doing as we wish. Until now you haven't arrived at the goal, the resting place, the inheritance that GOD, your God, is giving you. But the minute you cross the Jordan River and settle into the land GOD, your God, is enabling you to inherit, he'll give you rest from all your surrounding enemies. You'll be able to settle down and live in safety."*

God has chosen us to be different, set apart, PECULIAR: *"For thou art an holy people unto the LORD thy God, and the LORD hath chosen thee to be a peculiar people unto Himself above all the nations that are upon the earth."* **Deuteronomy 14:2 (KJV)**

He has also chosen us to be SEPARATE: *"Wherefore, come out from among them, and be ye separate, saith the Lord and touch not the unclean thing, and I will receive you."***2 Corinthians 6:17 (KJV)**

Let's look at what 'marching to the beat of God's drum looks like.

The word "march" is synonymous with "proceed" or "progress."

"Dance": 2 Samuel 6:21

"Drum": Psalm 150:1

Spiritual Identity

*"In a word, what I'm saying is, Grow up. You're kingdom subjects. Now live like it. Live out your God-created **identity**. Live generously and graciously toward others, the way God lives toward you."* **Matthew 5:48 (MSG)**

Stop trying to be like others or conforming so that others are comfortable. You have been designed with a purpose in mind. God has not made you to be like others, nor has He intended you to be the same. No longer allow the spirit of control from others to control your life's choices, decisions, actions or thoughts. A byproduct of this type of behavior is low self-esteem and fear. Well Beloved, God has NOT given us the spirit of fear, but a spirit of power, love and of a sound mind![35]

This is important because of all of the reasons we have discussed. All that is left is to ask yourself is the following:

Do I have the courage to be the person God created me to be?

_____

_____

_____

Take the first step to becoming her now. Answer these questions, and have the courage to be YOU:

What do you like?

_____

What do you think (about anything)?

_____

Can you make a decision without asking everyone to help you decide?

_____

Where do you want to go?

_____

Why can't you do that?

_____

_____

Says who? _____

As I was completing the section above, I heard the Holy Spirit say, "_spiritual robots._" Wow, what does that mean?

> **Robot:** An efficient, insensitive person who responds automatically, repetitively and lacks human emotions.

> **Spiritual:** A deeply emotional or deep emotional character or ecclesiastical (of or relating to the Christian church).

---

[35] 2 Timothy 1:7

In essence, a spiritual robot is someone who has a form of godliness, but they deny the power therein.[36] They do everything right in terms of acting in a way that looks Christian or speaking in a way that implies they are Christian. ***This person is simply 'religious', but not spiritual.***

An example of this is someone who is an active member of a church body (i.e. a member of the usher board, choir, hospitality, etc.). There is nothing wrong with being active. The problem lies in this person who comes to church, does their duty, speaks like a Christian, and then goes about their daily living in defeat, lacking faith or satisfying their flesh.

A spiritual robot has no prayer life, may speak negatively, is ineffective in reaching the high spiritual heights that God has called us to, believes the Word as it is told to them and never looks to confirm, learn or understand for themselves. Spiritual robots don't believe in or operate under the unction, anointing or guidance of the Holy Spirit of God and therefore, they have no power. They are normally not alone. They congregate in groups and try to entrap other believers who are unawares, weak in their faith or shaky in their walk with Christ.

Do you know anyone like this? Is this you? _____

The Proverbs 31 woman did her thing. She was led by God in all that she did and was not distracted, deluded or lost when it came to the things of God. Just as she did, purpose in your heart that you will be a **BOLD, POWER FILLED, LOVE FILLED, HOLY GHOST LED BELIEVER.**

Determine to march to the beat of God's drum and dance to your own rhythm.

Finally, **Romans 8:14 (NIV)** tells us, *"For those who are led by the Spirit of God are the children of God.*

Don't Back Down!

I was nearly finished with this entire book when I had an incident that the Lord led me to include. I had an opportunity to teach a course with a local, well-known and very well respected institution of higher learning. Well, I thought this is just the cat's meow! Here I am Dr. Patrice J. Carter and I am going to be teaching a course here?! I have finally arrived!

In preparation for the event, I decided that I would introduce myself using a slideshow presentation of pictures, as I had seen another speaker do. I cannot completely recall the order of the slides; however, they mentioned that I loved God, was a consultant and motivational speaker, married with a 12-year-old, etc.

[36]2 Timothy 3:5

The day of the class came and I introduced myself, I taught the course, read over the course feedback (and received pretty good comments) and turned in my materials. Three days later, I received a call from the point of contact. She wanted to discuss my course feedback.

"I received an email this weekend from one of your students and, it is very important that I share that with you first," she said. "Now, don't let this ruin your day."

The student (all adults, mind you) started out by stating that this particular institution is known for it's academic rigor and excellence and that she was concerned, after taking my course, about the consistency of this reputation as it relates to my instruction. She was especially incensed that I would dare to mention God in my introduction of myself, as opposed to my credentials. Furthermore, my introduction of my Christian beliefs led her to believe that this course was not so much what it was originally intended but was more of a sermon. Mind you, I only mentioned God ONCE. She suggested that this institution should be more careful in the future regarding the types of instructors they hire, etc.

Wow!

Upon completion, the point of contact asked me what my thoughts were. Needless to say, nothing I said was going to make a difference. I say this because, the point of contact was a born again believer just like I was and knew in advance what my slides were. However, she was in an awkward position and someone had to take the blame. Can you guess who?

This was a hard test. I say this because, of course, pride wanted to well up. I am a PhD and have been teaching for well over 11 years. However, it wasn't about that. The devil was angry that I took the time to give God glory for placing me at such an institution. How dare I?

Initially, it did ruin my day, but over time I realized if we say that we profess Christ and we want to reign with Him, we have to also be willing to suffer with Him and be willing and prepared to be *persecuted for Christ's sake.*

Matthew 5:10 (MSG) states, *"You're blessed when your commitment to God provokes persecution. The persecution drives you even deeper into God's kingdom."*

Lastly, the Word of God tells us, *"endure suffering along with me, as a good soldier of Christ Jesus."* **2 Timothy 2:3 (NLT)**

As you can imagine, I shared varied comments when I shared this scenario with people I know. A number of people said, "Well, we have to be aware of our surroundings and it isn't always wise to mention God." So basically, I got what I deserved.

Well, the devil is a liar and a defeated foe!

Who sets up a light and hides it under a bushel? I should be quiet so that others can be comfortable? I have to keep my good news to myself for fear of offense? God forbid!

It is time for us, as Believers, to take a stand! My father said, "If you deny Him, then He will deny you." I refuse to let my living be in vain - even if means I won't be invited back or I get put out. When it is all said in done, I have a home; my place is already prepared, according to **John 14:2**.

Where do you need to take a stand for God?

_____

_____

_____

_____

Are you worshipping Him in secret or out in the open?

_____

_____

_____

I will not back down and I encourage you not to either.

"*'No weapon that is formed against you will prosper; and every tongue that accuses you in judgment you will condemn. This is the heritage of the servants of the LORD, and their vindication is from me,' declares the LORD.*" **Isaiah 54:17 (NASB)**

LET ME HEAR YOUR WAR CRY!

Finances

Need Money? What's In Your Hands?

One day my son and I were in the car waiting for our turn in the teller line at the bank, and he said to me, "I need to find a way to make some money." My son is an amazing artist and has an affinity for graffiti art. I mentioned to him a year prior that he should perfect his art, and we would put it on t-shirts and sell them at the flea market over the summer. He could start his own business and not have to work a traditional summer job. Well, like most pre-teens, he just blew me off.

But this conversation got me to thinking, how many of us are sitting somewhere right now trying to figure out how we can take on another part time job or who can we call to borrow money from?

You have money in your hands! You don't believe me? God has given each one of us gifts, the problem is we fail to use them time and time again. We go and work jobs that we hate, that are mediocre and unfulfilling, because we fear doing the thing we love or are too lazy to try or don't believe that we can actually make a living at our craft. Well, I'm here to prove otherwise.

We consider our dreams and talents to be pipe dreams and some of us have even let others persuade us to believe there is no hope – or money - in doing what we love. I *love* to write, talk, and help people. This translates into me being an author, motivational speaker and consultant. I am not, at the time of this book, making major money doing these things. However, I am living my dream, believing God, speaking life and am building daily. I'm walking in faith and me and my family is wealthy in mind, body spirit and finances, in Jesus' name!

Come and go with me!

Take a moment to read Matthew 25: The Story About Investment.

You are in *total* error when you take your natural gifts; talents and abilities for granted and fail to use them for God's glory and for your good instead.

Here are a few REAL examples you may relate to:

Stephen was struggling financially. He has a natural gift for cooking the most amazing food. God told him to take this gift and use it, but he looked at all of the natural obstacles in his way as opposed to looking and asking God to show him the way spiritually, so that he could believe. God said, "I will bless it." Stephen never did it and continues to struggle financially and is now in disobedience.

Pray as Elijah prayed in **2 Kings 6: 17 (NIV):** *"Open his eyes, LORD, so that he may see. Then the LORD opened the servant's eyes, and he looked and saw the hills full of horses and chariots of fire all around Elisha."*

Tanisha has a natural ability to do hair. She is now using this ability in the midst of a financial crisis in her life and God is blessing her as a result of her obedience and faith in Him.

Marlissa has a natural affinity and love of babysitting. She is currently without a car, but people bring their babies to her to keep, and she is making money in the comfort of her own home.

Me: I am writing this book as God has told me to do and when I finish it, He has promised to bless me.

What work has God blessed your hands to do?

_____

_____

What do you love to do?

_____

_____

_____

What are you going to do about it?

_____

_____

_____

How can you make money doing it?

_____

_____

_____

STOP RIGHT NOW!

Do not put another obstacle - mental, emotional or otherwise – in your own way or allow anyone else to either!

There are some actions that must be taken on your part to be successful:

Step 1: You must pay God first – tithes *and* offerings. You *must* give Him your first fruits.

Have you done this? _____

Step 2: Recognize and use your talents.

What talent(s) do you have?

_____

_____

_____

Step 3: Work the Word. **Philippians 4:19 (KJV)** states: *"But my **God shall supply** all your need according to his riches in glory by Christ Jesus."*

Step 4: You must be a good steward. *"Whoever can be trusted with very little can also be trusted with much, and whoever is dishonest with very little will also be dishonest with."* **Luke 16:10 (NIV)**

Are you faithful and committed? _____

Holes In My Pockets!

In the night season of writing this book, I can honestly say that my husband and I, as well as other fellow laborers, were definitely in a tight space financially. I want to call it lack, as there was a lack of our "wants" being met; however, I would dishonor God by using that term, as there was no lack of "needs" being met. God has and continues to meet *every* single need. A good friend of mine put it like this: "We are not in lack, we are in transition"; meaning some "things" had to be purged, pruned and let go in order for us to move forward, however, basic life needs were NEVER neglected under the watchful care of our loving Father. Thank you God!

"That's not to say that times weren't scary," my friend added. "But know that fearful events are an exercise in faith stretching."

I didn't see it this way initially. However, as time went on, God opened my eyes and allowed me to see. My husband and I would look at each other at times and wonder why are we in lack? We pay our tithes, we give to the poor and needy, we try as much as possible to be led by the Spirit of God in our dealings, so what was really going on?

God revealed to us, that He was in fact supplying all of our needs according to His riches in glory by Christ Jesus; He was simply not supplying and coddling our flesh as we wanted. Why should He give us anything else when all we were doing was sitting around wondering and complaining about how we were so in lack and we didn't have the money to buy the computer we wanted, or the iPhone or the clothes? I bet God was saying, "Give me a break!" Or worse, "How long will I contend with these people who complain against me!"

136

Thousands - 200,000 to be exact - of the Israelites died in the wilderness as a result of complaining against God.   We repented and fast!

The other issue that we were guilty of was i-r-r-e-s-p-o-n-s-i-b-l-i-t-y. This was a painful, but true reality. We had made poor business decisions and entered into agreements that were not of God; used our credit cards unwisely; spent endlessly on stuff (clothes, shoes, purses, etc.). We had to have a "come to Jesus" moment with ourselves and with God and just accept the fact that we were the ones to blame for a portion of our financial dilemma and with the help of God we would do our part to change. Why was this *so* important?

"Whoever can be trusted with very little can also be trusted with much, and whoever is dishonest with very little will also be dishonest with much. **"Luke 16:10 (NIV)**

Take a moment to honestly assess yourself in light of your current financial situation.

On a different note, there were those around us who were seriously in lack. I know this because many would come to me and ask me for prayer, advice or just to have a shoulder to cry on. I wondered about this.

Many times I asked them all the same questions to help them get to the root of their situations:

- **Have you given your life to Christ?** If you don't belong to God, He is not responsible for you. In fact, you belong to the devil. This is harsh but it's true. There is no "in between," Beloved.[37]

- **Do you pay your tithes and offerings?** Will a man rob God?[38]

- **Are you doing what God has told you to do with your life and for Him?**[39] When we go out to do the work of God, we have all that we need in the form of the Holy Spirit and the power we receive from God as a result. In **Matthew 10:7**, Jesus sent the disciples out with only a staff, they had no money, no food, no luggage and no clothing. They were to depend solely on the kindness of strangers.

- **Are there any un-confessed sins in your life?**[40]

- **Have you given up that which is precious to you, or are you at least willing to do so?** [41]

---

[37]Romans 10:9
[38]Malachi 3:8
[39]John 14:15
[40]Psalm 66:18
[41]Matthew 19:16-22 and Genesis 22:1-2

- **Are you humble? Do you foster relationships with your fellow brothers and sisters?** You are part of a larger body and not an island unto yourself. Relationship, humility and unity are critical.[42]
- **Are you being a good steward over what God has given you?**

As a child of God, sometimes, we are just going to have to go through some things. God is glorified in this and we are strengthened.[43]

The Word of God tells us that true wealth is measured in service to the Kingdom of God, as opposed to one's wealth or status.

So, I ask are you truly in lack? If so, ask yourself why. Use the questions above, pray and seek God and wait for His response. His Word says, *"If any of you lacks wisdom, he should ask God, who gives generously to all without finding fault, and it will be given to him."* **James 1:5 (NIV)**

FINAL THOUGHTS...

- Pay your tithes and offerings with a grateful heart. **2 Corinthians 9:7**
- Stop complaining immediately! **Lamentations 3:39**
- Give to the poor, the needy, the widow and the orphaned; this is the will of God.
- **Proverbs 19:17**
- Stop being selfish, greedy and covetous with your stuff or your money! Realize that one day, you are going to die and you CANNOT take it with you when you are gone. **Matthew 6:19**
- Know what God's Word says regarding your situation.
- Be a good steward over what God has given you, regardless of the amount and regardless of your salary, circumstances or situation.
- **Prayerfully read Proverbs 31:13-22**

---

[42] 1 Corinthians 12:24
[43] 1 Peter 4:1-19

Before we complete this journey, there are a few more issues we have to address.

Be Who You Are

- Don't compare yourself to others;[44]
- Run your own race.[45]

Many Believers struggle with making comparisons. As you read this, you may think, "Not me." I beg to differ. We've all done it at some point in our life and some of us are doing it even now. What I have found is that we tend to compare ourselves situationally. By this, I mean we are fine until we are placed in a situation where, we feel inadequate, insecure or less than in some way. We get angry because we internally blame the other person(s) for making us feel this way, when in fact it is our own feeling(s) of failure or inadequacy that is fueling this negative emotion.

A friend of mine recently attended a conference comprised of "experts" in an industry he wanted to break into. The first seminar he attended was made up of industry people, who were jaded, bitter, and I dare say, prideful. As a result of this, my friend, who already struggled with feelings of inadequacy and the spirit of offense, was bothered and agitated by these attitudes.

I immediately sensed the hand of the enemy at work, and recognized that my friend was fighting with his old foes/feelings. This was and is a recipe for disaster for the believer!

I can personally relate to these feelings as I was someone who, for years, battled insecurity, low self-esteem, the spirit of "doubt" and it's sister spirit "confusion". I constantly compared myself to others. What a debacle! No matter how many degrees I had obtained or how much money I earned; how beautiful others told me I was; I *never* felt "good enough", smart enough, or pretty enough. I *always* felt as though I was behind the power curve and *everyone* always knew more than me and were always a step ahead of me.

In addition to this head-trip, I was filled with the doubt and confusion of, "Have I missed God? Am I doing something wrong? Should I be doing something different? I don't have the money to do that. I wonder what **(fill in the blank)** thinks?"

JUST STOP IT! I mean, this seriously could go on FOREVER!

---

[44] Galatians 6:4

[45] Hebrews 12:1

Galatians 6:4 (NIV) tells us not to compare ourselves to others, but to test our own actions; **Hebrews 12:1 (NIV) gives** great advice: *"Run your own race."*

Also, the finish line is not here on earth any way; it's in HEAVEN! However, we each have our own individual lane and journey. Think of how disastrous it can be when cars start crossing over into other lanes!

I have *finally* decided (and I pray that you will also) that we simply must run our own race. We spend too much time trying to be like other people or do what other people do, when it may not even be God's plan for us and as a result, we miss our own journey and blessings. The experience of running our race, striving, falling, hurting, being short of breath, it is all GRACE and it is part of the process. The clothes, the shoes, the distance have all been individually assigned and ordained JUST FOR YOU by God and He has equipped us thusly for our own individual race and individual success. We will not be successful trying to do this with someone else's equipment on someone else's track.

As my friend was heading back into one of his conference sessions, I reminded him, and I'm reminding you, people 'front' all the time. For those PhDs reading this, that means, to pretend or fake it. People pretend all of the time to be more successful, more wealthy, more whatever than they truly are. Why is this? Because, they too, are insecure, filled with self-doubt, and guilty of comparing themselves. My friend came back that evening and shared with me how many of these same individuals were recently laid off of work and dissatisfied with life.

This tells us that no matter, where we are, what we have, who we are, when we are, we all experience these negative emotions and we simply MUST STOP!

Repeat after me: "Thank God to the praise of the glory of his grace, wherein he has made us accepted in the beloved, in Jesus' name."

You are good enough for God through His grace. HALLELUJAH!

What does this really mean?

I AM GOOD ENOUGH....YOU ARE GOOD ENOUGH!

NOW...GO AND LIVE IT! GO AND SHARE IT!

BE WHO YOU ARE: ACCEPT YOU AND LOVE YOU!

Proverbs 31:29 (NIV) tells us, *"Many women do noble things, but you surpass them all."*

Welcome Home

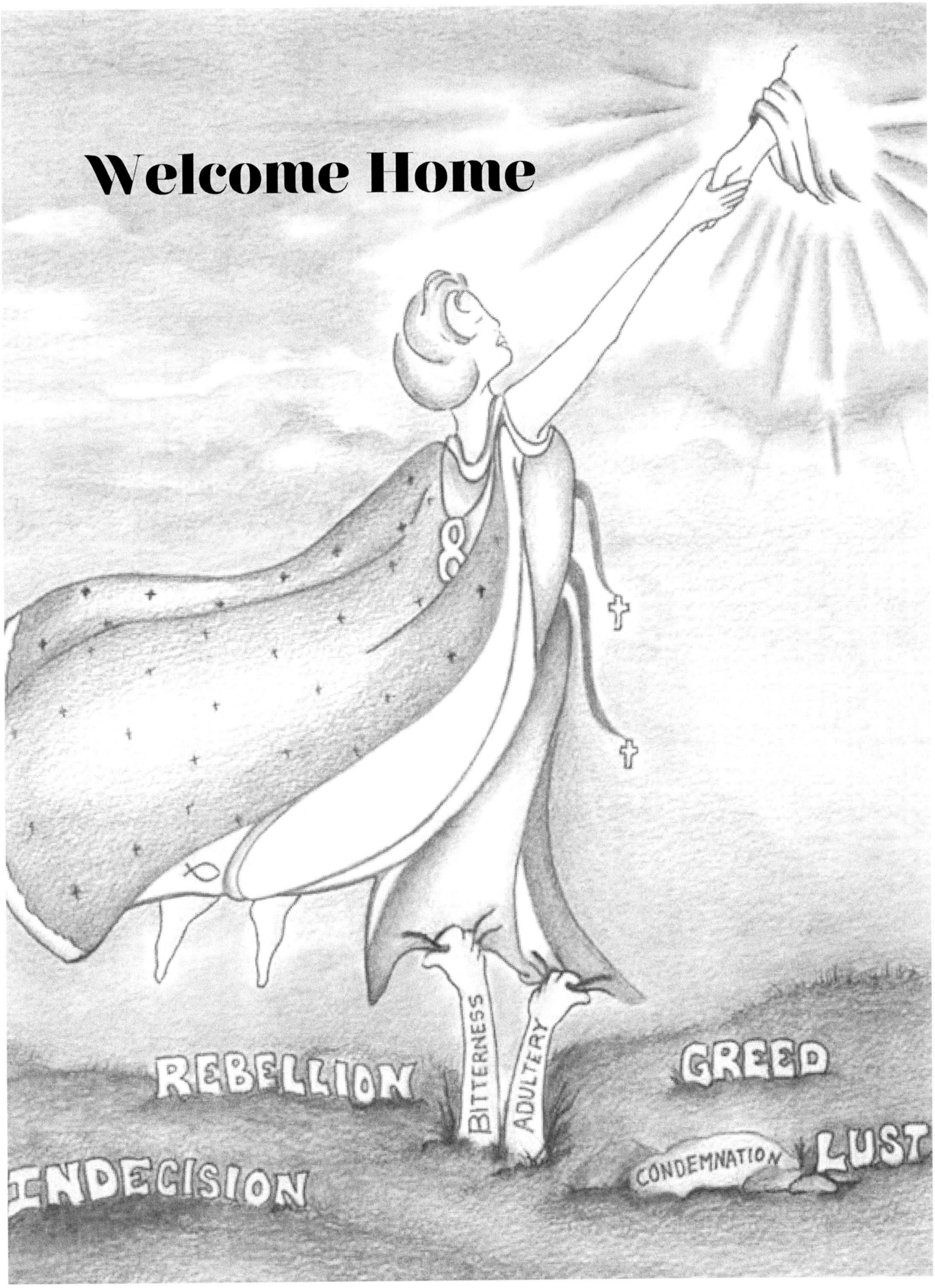

There's No Place Like Home!

Beloved, you have spent enough time, years, maybe a lifetime in the wilderness. There, you have experienced slavery, release, slavery again, giants, enemies, attacks, loss, pain, trials, separation, illness, death and divorce.

It is time to come out of your wilderness and into your promised land. What has God promised you? The path God is calling you to is the place of promise, filled with His peace, fullness of joy, there are pleasures at His right hand forevermore.[46] Now that you know there is a better place, won't you return to Him? **Do you still believe a "bad" girl cannot become God's girl?**

I beg to differ…

God has been calling you ALL along. That empty place within you that was and is always empty that left you feeling as though something is missing; the one you tried to fill with love (a.k.a. lust); drugs, alcohol, makeup, education, shopping, *(fill in the blank)*; that's the place only God can fill. The place in you is His place that can ONLY be filled by Him and no one or thing can or will ever be able to make it whole.

God is saying, *"But whoever takes a drink of the water that I will give him shall never, no never, be thirsty any more. But the water that I will give him shall become a spring of water welling up (flowing, bubbling) [continually] within him unto (into, for) eternal life."* **John 4:14 (AMP)**

You are *so* weary and you have toiled in places that God has not assigned, destined, or sent you to. You took your own way… and now, He desires to show you the way, back home to Him. Leave *everything* now and follow Him.

There is a wonderful parable in the Bible that many of us are familiar with, the Prodigal Son in **Luke 5:11-32**. I will let you read this on your own, however, I want to focus your attention on verse 17; the son came to his senses and realized that he was better off with the Father. Having realized this, he determines in his heart the conversation/conversion he will have with his Father.

"When he came to his senses, he said, 'How many of my father's hired men have food to spare, and here I am starving to death! I will set out and go back to my father and say to him: Father, I have sinned against heaven and against you. I am no longer worthy to be called your son; make me like one of your hired men.' So he got up and went to his father." **Luke 5:17-20 (NIV)**

---
[46] Psalm 16:11

This is the part that just makes me want to holler!

"So he got up and went to his father. But while he was still a long way off, his father saw him and was filled with compassion for him; he ran to his son, threw his arms around him and kissed him." **Luke 5:20 (NIV)**

He went to his father and his father, who had every right to be bitter, angry, and mad saw His son, ran to him, threw His arms around him and kissed him. Don't you see? God is waiting for YOU to come to your senses, come home to him and be welcomed with compassion, open arms, kisses and hugs. HE'S WAITING ON YOU!

"Next, the son repented saying, 'Father, I have sinned against heaven and against you. I am no longer worthy to be called your son.' But the father said to his servants, 'Quick! Bring the best robe and put it on him. Put a ring on his finger and sandals on his feet. Bring the fattened calf and kill it. Let's have a feast and celebrate. For this son of mine was dead and is alive again; he was lost and is found.' So they began to celebrate." **Luke 5:21-24 (NIV)**

You too are dead; you too are lost. But when you decide to give your life to Jesus; to return to your first love- God; you will LIVE AGAIN and you WILL BE FOUND. Jesus says in **Luke 15:7 (NIV)**; *"I tell you that in the same way there will be more rejoicing in heaven over one sinner who repents than over ninety-nine righteous persons who do not need to repent."*

How will you know when you are home? In the natural sense, home looks different to everyone. However, as a child of God, you will know, within your spirit, you are home when you experience the following fruit of the Spirit: love, joy, peace, forbearance, kindness, goodness, faithfulness, gentleness and self-control.[47]

Prayer: *Father, in the name of Jesus, I repent for the times I walked away from you; for the sins I committed wandering in the wilderness. I want to come back home to the safety and love of your arms; receive me now and restore me, in Jesus' name I pray. Amen.*

WELCOME HOME MY DAUGHTER! You are no longer called by the name you had at the beginning. I now call you MINE, God's Girl. I LOVE YOU AND RECEIVE YOU!

Love,

Your Father, God ∞

---

[47] Galatians 5:22-23

HERE I AM! GOD'S GIRL!

INSERT PHOTOGRAPH OF YOUR TRANSFORMED SELF HERE

"Our soul has escaped as a bird from the snare of the fowlers; the snare is broken, and we have escaped." **Psalm 124:7 (NKJV)**

"In my Father's house are many rooms; if it were not so, I would have told you. I am going there to prepare a place for you" **John 14:2 (NIV)**

Prayer Journal

Throughout this entire journey home, we have relied upon the Word of God and prayer. You must commit to keeping these up as a daily practice. There is power in praying the Word of God.

Thessalonians 5:17 (KJV) states that we should pray without ceasing and **Luke 18:1 (KJV)** states that men ought always to pray, and not faint. This is so true. There is power in the Word of God. If you were to study the Word of God, you would come across multiple instances where the disciples, prophets and others prayed and God responded to each of their prayers with power, might, urgency, completeness.

Many people already have a prayer life; however, we could all use an increase in the power and specificity of our prayers. How can this be accomplished? God, in **Isaiah 55:11 (KJV)** states, *"So shall My word be that goeth forth out of my mouth; it shall not return unto me void, but it shall accomplish that which I please, and it shall prosper in the thing whereto I sent it."*

There is POWER in praying the Word of God. I would like for you to pray for 50 days. Most people say 30 or 40 but 50 is the number of Jubilee - God's restoration. God's restoring to us all that was stolen, double portion; a season of restoration; emancipation -freedom. Set your heart on what you want to see God manifest on Day 50 and EXPECT HIM TO MOVE! More importantly, watch the powerful manifestations of your prayers daily as you seek Him and as you pray His Word.

Below is an example of how to pray the Word of God:

Malachi 3:10-13 Prayer for Finances

"Dear Heavenly Father, I come to you now in the name of my Lord and Savior, Jesus Christ. Holy Spirit, I welcome you and ask that you make intercession for me to God, according to His perfect will. Father, you said in your Word in Malachi 3:10 that if I would bring all of my tithes into the storehouse, that there may be food in your house; then I could try you in this and you would open up the windows of heaven and pour out for me such a blessing that there would not be room enough to receive it and that You would rebuke the devourer for my sake, so that he will not destroy the fruit of my ground, nor shall the vine fail to bear fruit for me in the field; and all nations would call me blessed and I will be a delightful land. I bring you in remembrance of Your Word concerning me and ask that, as I tithe, you move according to this Word in my finances and in my life in Jesus' name. Amen."

Now you try it. Pick a scripture or verse pertaining to an area in your life (i.e. healing, deliverance, salvation, finances, etc.) that you need God to move and pray it according to His Word.

Proverbs 31: Daily Prayer Journal

Remember to pray these daily and to pray the Word of God. It may feel awkward at first; however, the more you practice, the better you will be. I will help you with some and then it's up to you. Please don't quit now. This is about discipline and going to the next level in prayer.

Day 1: Romans 10:9

God in Heaven, I come to you in the name of Jesus. I confess I have not lived my life for you. But I am glad to know I can change that. According to your Word in Romans 10:9, I have decided to accept that Jesus is your son, and that He died on the cross and rose again from the dead, so I might have eternal life and the blessings of life now. Jesus come into my heart, be my Savior, be my Lord. From this day forward, and to the best of my ability, I will live my life for you. In Jesus' name I pray. Amen.

Day 2: Proverbs 31:10-31

Father in the name of Jesus, I come to you with a praise of thanksgiving on my lips. Thank you for your Holy Spirit, whom I welcome in and submit my will to; and thank you for Your Son Jesus who died that I might live. Heavenly Father, my prayer is that you would help me to become the woman that you have called me to be according to your Words in Proverbs 31 verses 10-31. Help me to become a woman and wife of noble character, bless me so that my husband will have full confidence in me and will lack nothing of value; bless me to do him good and not harm all the days of our life; bless me to work prosperously with my hands, time, talent and abilities and to be an excellent mother and prosperous business woman; Father, I fear you and ask that you let me be praised, blessed and highly favored, by You and by man, according to Your Word, in Jesus' name. Amen.

Day 3: Matthew 6:33

Dear Heavenly Father, help me to live according to your Word in Matthew 6:33; help me to seek first Your Kingdom and Your righteousness God that ALL things might be added unto me, according to Your Word. Show me Father, what you would have me to do and then strengthen me to do it; then bless me with all that you have for me, in Jesus' name, I pray. Amen.

Day 4: Isaiah 61:1-2

Father, I come to you know in the name of Jesus and ask the Holy Spirit to help me to hear your voice and to make intercession for me. Heavenly Father, I ask according to your Word in Isaiah 61 that you would help me to get busy, that as Jesus did, you would anoint me to preach good news to the poor; heal the brokenhearted; announce freedom to all those who are bound; and forgive and pardon all prisoners and to announce the acceptable year of the Lord, vengeance to our enemies and comfort to all who mourn, in Jesus' name, I pray. Amen.

Day 5: Galatians 5:13

Father in the name of Jesus, I come to say thank you, thank you Jesus for setting me free! I pray Father God that I would, according to Your Word, not use my freedom as an opportunity to sin, rather that through your love, I would serve others. Holy Spirit, show me how to love my neighbor and my family as myself and to stop backbiting, gossiping and being consumed or overrun by other people, in Jesus' name I pray. Amen.

Day 6: Galatians 5:1-25

Father in the name of Jesus, I ask you in the name of Jesus and in the power of the Holy Spirit to help me. Help me God to clean up my life. Help me Holy Spirit to run a good race, a race pleasing to God and to get rid of anyone who is not of God and who will or has caused me to stumble. Forgive me for wanting to get my way all of the time and help me to submit my will to God and to walk in the fruit of the Spirit which are, joy, peace, longsuffering, kindness, goodness, faithfulness, gentleness, and self-control, against such there is no law and I put away any forms of sin **(state them out loud)** in my life. In Jesus' name I pray. Amen.

Day 7: Matthew 4:4

Father, in the name of Jesus and in the power of your Word, I ask you to help me Holy Spirit to not try and live by human bread alone, but to live according the Word of God. I submit my life to the Word of God and ask that as I study and learn that you give me wisdom to know His Word and the ability to apply it to my life in Jesus' name. Amen.

Day 8: Matthew 5:14; Matthew 5:16

Father in the name of Jesus and through the power of the Holy Spirit help me to live my life as Jesus did; as a light to men so that others will see my good works and glorify you, according to Matthew 5:14 and Matthew 5:16; help me not hide Your light in me because of fear or laziness, but to shine brightly that everyone may see you. In Jesus' name I pray. Amen.

Day 9: Jeremiah 29:11

Father in the name of Jesus I thank you, in the name of Jesus and ask that you help me to stand on your Word. Your Word in Jeremiah 29:11 states that you know the plans you have for us, plans to prosper us and not harm us, plans to give us hope, a future and an expected end. I receive it and stand on it, in Jesus Holy name. Thank you and amen!

Day 10: Ephesians 5:25

Heavenly Father, in the name of Jesus, please help me through your Holy Spirit to have Godly expectations regarding what to expect from my husband (or future husband). According to Your Word in Ephesians 5:25, incline my husband to go all out for me as Christ did for the church and to let his love for me be marked by giving and not getting. Let His love make me whole as Christ's love for us has made us whole and let him speak life over me and clothe me in holiness. Father let his love be your love and let me receive it as such, in Jesus' name. Amen.

Day 11: Ephesians 5:24

Father God, as the Church submits to Christ, so also let me as be a wife who submits to to my husband in everything. Help me to follow Him as he follows Christ, in Jesus' name. Amen.

Day 12: Genesis 19:22

Father, in the name of Jesus and through the power of the Holy Spirit, I pray that when you command me to move and to go in a direction that you send me, I will NOT question you, but I will obey your Word that I might have life. In Jesus' name I pray. Amen.

Day 13: Genesis 24:58-60

Father, in the name of Jesus, help me to receive all that you have for me, especially the husband you have for me, that I may increase to thousands upon thousands and my offspring may possess the gates of my enemies. In Jesus' name, I pray. Amen.

Day 14: Hosea 2:15

Father God, I pray in the name of Jesus, that as you did in Hosea 2:15, you would take me back to the place where we first met; and show me that you are my true husband, not the things of this world that I have married myself to, clean me up and clean me out, especially my mouth, that I might be redeemed and then God, marry me again and restore me back to you as your bride, the church. I thank you God, in Jesus' name.

Day 15: Exodus 32:26-27

Father in the name of Jesus and through the power of your Holy Spirit, I vow that I am with you, God; I am on Your side. I pray that you will help me to put to death any unholy associations, agreements and relationships with those that are not of you, regardless of their relationship to me, in Jesus' name. Amen.

Day 16: Hebrews 13:12

Father God, in Hebrews 13:12, that I have been set apart and that part of this being set apart, requires that I must suffer also as Christ suffered. Please help me through the power of the Holy Spirit to endure as Jesus endured that I too might receive my place in your Kingdom, in Jesus' name I pray. Amen.

Day 17: 1 Corinthians 16:9

Father God, according to your Words in 1 Corinthians 6:9, a huge door of opportunity has opened for me in the spiritual realm and also huge demonic opposition as a result. I thank you for this opportunity and pray also according to the Isaiah 54:17 that no weapon that is formed against me shall prosper in Jesus' name. Amen.

Day 18: Colossians 4:3

Father, in the name of Jesus and according to Your Word in Colossians 4:3, I ask the Holy Spirit to help me to pray diligently and to help me to stay alert with my eyes wide open in gratitude. I pray for those who are bound, physically, mentally, emotionally and spiritually; and, I pray that every time I open my mouth, I will make Christ as plain as day to believers and unbelievers alike, in Jesus' name. Amen.

154

Day 19: Matthew 16:18

Father, in the name of Jesus, as Simon Peter did, help me through the power of the Holy Spirit to see you for myself; and, as you did in Matthew 16:18, let me in on the secret of who you really are and make me a rock, on which you can establish your church, so expansive with energy that not even the gates of hell will be able to keep it out. In Jesus' name, I pray. Amen.

Day 20: John 10:7-9

Father, you said in Your Word that you are the Gate for the sheep. All those others are up to no good—sheep stealers, every one of them. But the sheep didn't listen to them. For you are the Gate. I acknowledge that I am Your sheep and that you are the Gate. Help me Holy Spirit to go through God so that I will be cared for and will go freely in and out and find pasture. The devil is a thief and only came to steal and kill and destroy. Thank you Daddy that you came so that I might have real and eternal life, more and better life than I ever dreamed of, in Jesus' name, I receive it, according to Your Word in John 10: 7-9. Amen.

Day 21: Revelation 4:1

Father according to Your Word in Revelation 4:1, I pray you will help me, through the power of the Holy Spirit, to ascend higher and that you will show me what happens next, in Jesus' name. Amen.

Day 22: Revelation 3:8

Father God, Your Word in Revelation 3:8, says, you see what I've done; and now I would see what you're going to do. Thank you God that you have opened a door before me that no one can slam shut. You know I don't have much strength and you know that; I used what I had to keep Your Word. I didn't deny you when times were rough and I thank you for all that I am about to receive in Jesus' name. Amen.

Day 23: Revelation 8:20

Father, you said in Your Word to look at You, that You stand at the door and knock; and if I hear you call to open the door. Father, I hear you and I open the door to you, the door to my heart, the door to my mind, the door to my body and the door to my soul and my emotions. Come in Daddy and sit down to supper with me. As a Conqueror, I will sit alongside You at the head table, just as You, Jesus, having conquered, took the place of honor at the side of the Father. Thank you for your gift to me as a Conqueror, in Jesus' name. Amen!

Day 24: Psalm 24:7

God according to Your Word, help me through the power of the Holy Spirit to lift up my head and lift up my gates that You Oh Lord may come in! Hallelujah! I invite you into my life, take your place at the head and rule me Lord God. You are strong and mighty in battle and I submit to you! Hallelujah! In Jesus' name, I pray. Amen!

Day 25 Psalm 100:4

Daddy, according to Your Word in Psalm 100 verse 4, I enter into Your gates with Thanksgiving and into Your court with praise. You are AWESOME and worthy of all my praise, in Jesus' name! I thank you! Amen.

Day 26: Psalm 107:16

Father, according to Your Word, we were locked in a dark cell, cruelly confined behind bars, Punished for defying Your Word, for turning our back on Your counsel— A hard sentence, and our hearts so heavy, and not a soul in sight to help. Then we called out to You in our desperate condition; You got us out in the nick of time. You led us out of our dark, dark cell, broke open the jail and led us out. So thank You God for Your marvelous love, for Your miracle mercy to the children You love; You shattered the heavy jailhouse doors, You snapped the prison bars like matchsticks. For this I say THANK YOU! Hallelujah! In Jesus' name, Amen.

Day 27: Psalm 141:3

Father, in the name of Jesus and through the power of the Holy Spirit, I ask you to set a guard over my mouth, O Lord, and keep watch over the door of my lips according to Psalm 141:3.

Day 28: Proverbs 12:4

Father, in Your Word in Proverbs 12:4, it states, "a hearty wife invigorates her husband, but a frigid woman is cancer in the bones". Help me through the power of the Holy Spirit to invigorate my husband, and forgive me for when I have been like a cancer to His bones, in Jesus' name, I pray. Amen.

Day 29: 1 Corinthians 11:3-9

Father, in the name of Jesus and according to Your Word in 1 Corinthians 11:3-9, I pray that you will help me to speak to you in the way a wife should. Help me to show respect for your authority and respect for my husband's authority. I yield and submit myself to you and ask Holy Spirit that you help me to show respect both in my attitude and my actions. Thank you God. Amen.

Day 30: Revelation 1:8

Father, in the name of Jesus and according to Your Word in Revelation 1:8, I acknowledge that you are Alpha and Omega, the beginning and the end, which is and was and which is to come, the Almighty. I praise you in Jesus' name. Amen.

Day 31: Colossians 3:19

Father in the name of Jesus and according to Your Word, bless my husband with the mind of Christ that He will go all out in His love for me; and that He will not take advantage of me, now or ever. Amen.

Day 32: Ephesians 5:33

Father, in the name of Jesus and by the power of the Holy Spirit, help my husband and me to cleave to one another and to love one another as you love the church, in Jesus' name. Amen

Day 33: 1 Peter 3:2

Father, in the name of Jesus, help me to cultivate my inner beauty. Also, help me to be a good wife to my husband, responsive to his needs. Let my husband be captivated by my life of holy beauty. What matters is not my outer appearance—the styling of my hair, the jewelry I wear, the cut of my clothes—but my inner disposition. Thank you God. Amen.

Day 34: Proverbs 13:12

Father, in Your Word in Proverbs 13:12, you said, that, *"hope deferred makes the heart sick, but when the desire comes, it is a tree of life."* Bless me God to realize my dreams God that I might be a tree of life; life to You, life to myself and life to all those around me, in Jesus' name, I pray. Amen.

Day 35: Philippians 1:6

Father God, thank you for Your Promise to me in Philippians 1:6, where You said, that You have begun a good work in me and would complete it until the day of Jesus Christ. Thank you for keeping Your Word and I submit to Your Good Work, in Jesus' name. Amen.

Day 36: Romans 12:2

Father according to Your Word in Romans 12:2, and through the power of the Holy Spirit, help me to not be conformed to this world, but to be transformed by the renewing of my mind that I may prove what is that good and acceptable and perfect will of you God, in Jesus' name, I pray. Amen.

Day 37: Philippians 4:1

Father in the name of Jesus and through the power of the Holy Spirit, I CAN do ALL things through Christ who gives me strength. Hallelujah!

Book Study and Bible Study Discussion Group Questions

1. Do you think the standards of the Proverbs 31 woman are achievable for today's woman? If not, why not? If so, what modifications have been made to the model?

2. How would she have encouraged her other sister-friends who were not able to do all that she did and have her family rise up and call her blessed?

3. How did she rear her male and female children differently?

4. That has often been a question in my mind also. I often cringed as many Pastors (mostly male) held up her as this impossible standard and wanted to know was there a comparable male figure (other than David - a man after God's own heart)?

5. What are some of the occurrences that led to Bathsheba's change? Can you relate?

6. Can women of today *truly* identify with Bathsheba with her reformed into the Proverbs 31 woman? Why or why not?

7. How do we not place ourselves in a position that we are doing so much for the family that we feel that WE are running the family and not our husband? How do we find that balance?

8. What is the significance of the number 8 on the SUPERb Woman's cape on the book cover?

9. What do the colors on her person represent?

10. Why is the SUPERb spelled with a lowercase "b"?

Note from the Author

This book has truly been a journey for me, a journey home, so that I could show you the way, show you how to avoid the pits I fell in and welcome you across the finish line- HOME.

There were times I wondered if I was meant to write this book, if I would finish this book, or if I would even say anything that would help someone reading it. The Holy Spirit reminded me that I could only write what I had lived and experienced, therefore, there were times I didn't write because I was living the chapter; or God was dealing with me about myself.

But God who is always faithful will complete the good work He has begun in us. I decided I wouldn't make another move on this book until God speaks, because each time I sat down to write, there was this huge blank wall—a mental block. Well praise God! My friend called me and said, "God dealt with me about you at 1:00 a.m. last night (thank God for saints who don't mind waking up to pray and are obedient to the voice of God!); and He told me to call you and tell you that you need to finish your book. The time is now!" Hallelujah!

I won't say that I didn't still feel the mental block or as though I was living some of the chapters; however, I had a renewed sense of purpose and desire to finish this book. I needed to finish it for me and my family's sake, but I really needed to finish it for YOU.

I love you and I believe in you. More than that, I believe God and His word concerning you.

Please email me at bcomegodsgirl@gmail.com to let me know your thoughts, feedback or comments regarding this book. Also, I want to know when you have "made it home safely."

Bibliography

Williamson, M. (1992). A return to love, 7, 190-191.

Anonymous. How to play follow the leader. Retrieved from
http://www.ehow.com/how_2074033_play-follow-leader.html

Merriam-Webster Dictionary. Retrieved from
http://www.merriam-webster.com/dictionary.

The New Strong's Concise Concordance & Vine's Dictionary of the Bible. (1997, 1999).
Thomas Nelson, Inc.

SUPERb Woman Products and Services

Now that you have completed your journey, let everyone know! We have the following SUPERb Woman items for sale!

- "I AM A SUPERb WOMAN" Bracelet

- "I AM A SUPERb WOMAN" T-shirt

- "I AM A SUPERb WOMAN" Logo Bag

- "I AM A SUPERb Woman" Coffee Mug

- "I AM A SUPERb Woman" Sticky Notes

- "I AM A SUPERb Woman" Pen

- Additional copies of SUPERb Woman: From Bad Girl to God's Girl $17.99 each, available at www.speaktotheworld.org and www.drpatricecarter.com.
- Audio book version of SUPERb Woman: From Bad Girl to God's Girl, available at www.speaktotheworld.org and www.drpatricecarter.com (COMING SOON)
- E-book version of SUPERb Woman: From Bad Girl to God's Girl is available at www.speaktotheworld.org and www.drpatricecarter.com. (COMING SOON)

- SUPERb Woman Conferences and Speaking Engagements

To schedule Dr. Carter to speak to your organization or to place an order, send an, email to her at bcomegodsgirl@gmail.com or call (910) 551-7358. Check out her calendar of events and book tour dates on www.bcomegodsgirl.com!

THANK YOU FOR YOUR SUPPORT!